W9-AFZ-777

HISTORICAL FACTS

ANCIENT TIMES

Zapotec pottery cremation urn, from Monte Alban (Mexico), a
Zapotec 'city' or ceremonial center c.400 B.C.-c.A.D. 900.

The giant carved stone heads of Easter Island in the Pacific, made by an isolated people whose culture was wiped out 200 years ago, remain one of the mysteries of the ancient world.

Rome's Colosseum (A.D. 80) was the work of a highly developed civilization, who have left behind not only massive ruins but great literature as evidence.

HISTORICAL FACTS
ANCIENT TIMES

AMANDA O'NEILL

CRESCENT BOOKS
NEW YORK • AVENEL, NEW JERSEY

CLB 2836

© 1992 Colour Library Books Ltd., Godalming, Surrey, England.

All rights reserved

This 1992 edition published by Crescent Books,
distributed by Outlet Book Company, Inc.,
a Random House Company
40 Engelhard Avenue, Avenel, New Jersey 07001

Printed and bound in Italy

ISBN 0 517 06559 2

8 7 6 5 4 3 2 1

The Author
Amanda O'Neill was born in Sussex, England, in 1951, and studied Anglo-Saxon, Old Norse, and Middle English literature at the University of Exeter. Her specialist field of interest lies in the Celtic myths and medieval romances of King Arthur. She has edited and written books on topics ranging from the decorative arts to natural history, and is currently engaged in a study of the history of domesticated animals and their association with humans.

Credits
Editor: Richard O'Neill
Designer: Jill Coote
Map artwork: Peter Bull
Picture Editor: Miriam Sharland
Production: Ruth Arthur, Sally Connolly, Andrew Whitelaw
Director of Production: Gerald Hughes
Typesetting: SX Composing Ltd.
Color separations: Scantrans Pte Ltd., Singapore
Printed and bound by New Interlitho SpA, Italy

Stone Age monuments keep their secrets. Was the holed stone of Men-an-tol (Cornwall, England) an astronomer's instrument, aligned to measure sunrise, or a tomb's 'porthole' window to the world of the dead?

CONTENTS

Introduction

The ancient world was largely an unknown realm until the last century. Until c.A.D. 1800, historians' knowledge of the ancient world came largely from the works of that world's own historians, in which useful information is often inextricably entwined with myth, legend, and gossip, and facts are sometimes deliberately perverted to satisfy racial, social, political, or religious prejudices (not that all modern historians are guiltless in this respect). The Christian Bible and other religious works were the main sources of knowledge of the great civilizations existing in the Middle East long before the birth of Christ. All educated people were familiar (as they are not today, when the Greek and Latin 'classics' are no longer thought of as the beginning and end of education) with certain aspects of the civilizations of classical Greece and Rome, which left not only magnificent ruins but also great literature and artworks. But, Greece and Rome apart, thousands of years of human existence were generally dismissed, in the words of the 17th century philosopher Thomas Hobbes, as having had: 'No arts; no letters; no society . . . and the life of man, solitary, poor, nasty, brutish, and short.'

In the 19th century, a very different picture began to emerge through a

Under Emperor Augustus (ruled 27 B.C.-A.D. 14), Rome's writers – including Horace, Livy, Virgil, and Ovid – produced many of the works which were to be the 'classics' of later ages.

series of dramatic archaeological discoveries. The 1840s saw the discovery of Biblical Nineveh and the disclosure of the world of the Assyrians – known until then only from the Old Testament. Between the 1870s and early 1900s, two hitherto unknown prehistoric civilizations were discovered: the Mycenaean civilization of mainland Greece, and the Minoan civilization of Crete. Some 20 years later,

Stone Age architects made an artificial hill 130ft (39.6m) high, at Silbury (Wiltshire, England), that still holds its perfect conical shape.

investigation of sites at Mohenjo-Daro and Harappa in Pakistan revealed the existence of the Indus civilization, a culture far older than any previously believed to have existed on the Indian subcontinent. Archaeologists continue to uncover many more layers of the past. Modern researchers believe that the human species has existed on earth for some 250,000 years – and it is increasingly clear that the life of our ancient ancestors can no longer be dismissed as 'brutish.'

From 1836, archaeologists adopted a 'three-age system,' classifying ancient societies as Stone Age, Bronze Age, or Iron Age, according to their level of development. They theorized that the progress of ancient peoples towards 'civilization' (as represented by the Greeks and Romans) could be measured in terms of materials used. Stone Age humans had learned to make stone tools; Bronze Age humans had progressed to the use of copper and other metals; and Iron Age people had advanced as far as the discovery of the wonder metal, iron. These labels still form a useful way of grouping early cultures, although scholars now know that there was no simple, linear progression from primitive people chipping out crude stone tools to cultured societies practicing arts and sciences.

The 'first men' are now known to have been far more complex than was once thought. When archeologists first identified Neanderthal Man – one of the earliest human subspecies, who lived some 70,000-35,000 years ago – they saw him as a lumbering cretin, and for years denied his association with the stone tools found with his bones. This view has been drastically revised. Neanderthals are now known to have been tool-makers; their society had evolved as far as burying their dead with ceremony and supporting physically disadvantaged members of their communities – as proved by the remains, found in Iraq, of a Neanderthaler who, despite partial blindness, lameness, and an arm withered from childhood, reached the then considerable age of 40 years.

Thousands of carved seals for stamping goods attest to the prosperity of the Indus civilization (c.2500-1500 B.C.) – and are also miniature works of art.

Wall paintings, their colors still bright, depict scenes of elegant luxury enjoyed by the Minoan civilization of Crete (c.3000-1400 B.C.)

The Stone Age saw great technological advances by Neanderthaler's successors – in art, building, medicine (including surgery), mining, and industry (producing stone tools in quantity for trade). Even ocean-going boats were among the achievements of people once dismissed as 'cavemen.' A major revolutionary development was farming, which gave rise to self-supporting settlements rather than bands of roving hunters. From such settlements, in some parts of the world, the first cities had evolved by c.5000 B.C.

The move towards civilization, in its literal sense of 'city-dwelling,' began in the Middle East, in Mesopotamia (an area covered in detail in the companion volume to this book, *Biblical Times*). These early cities were in many ways startlingly 'modern,' from their government and legal codes to their paved streets and municipal sewage systems. It was probably the bureaucratic needs of urban life that produced the further major invention of writing. But 'barbarian' societies which did not adopt city-dwelling were no less cultured for the absence of tax collectors and town drains. The megalith builders of Europe, who raised great stone circles in the Late Stone Age, had a sophisticated calendar based on wide knowledge of astronomy, as well as the technical skill to move and erect the huge stones.

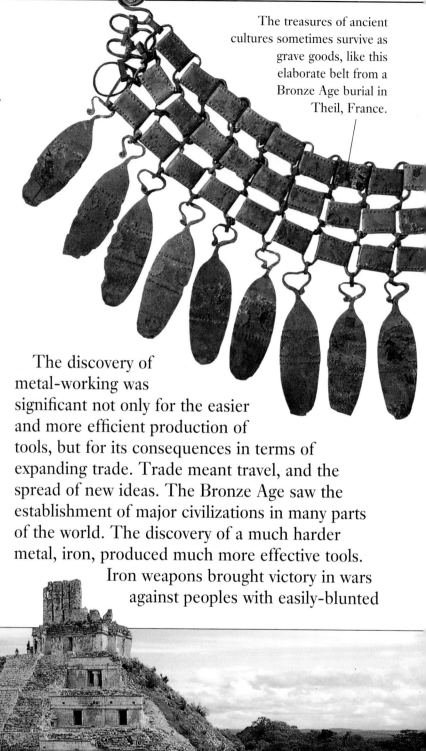

The treasures of ancient cultures sometimes survive as grave goods, like this elaborate belt from a Bronze Age burial in Theil, France.

The discovery of metal-working was significant not only for the easier and more efficient production of tools, but for its consequences in terms of expanding trade. Trade meant travel, and the spread of new ideas. The Bronze Age saw the establishment of major civilizations in many parts of the world. The discovery of a much harder metal, iron, produced much more effective tools. Iron weapons brought victory in wars against peoples with easily-blunted

The early peoples of Middle America developed their great civilizations independently of developments in other parts of the world. Without metal tools, the wheel, or even animal transport, they raised mighty buildings – like this temple-pyramid in Yucatan, Mexico. They also developed sophisticated astronomical and mathematical knowledge, accurate calendars, writing, and a durable political system.

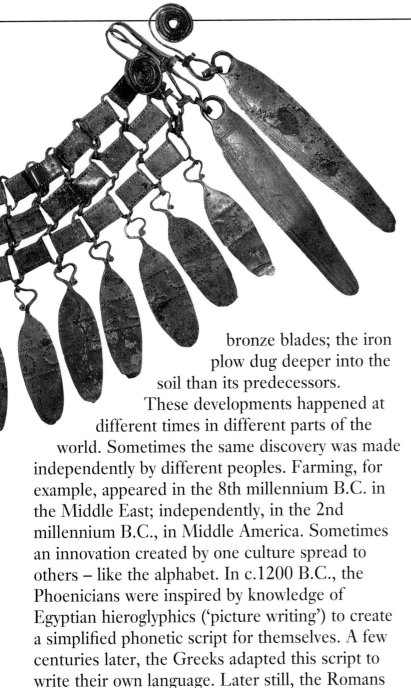

bronze blades; the iron plow dug deeper into the soil than its predecessors.

These developments happened at different times in different parts of the world. Sometimes the same discovery was made independently by different peoples. Farming, for example, appeared in the 8th millennium B.C. in the Middle East; independently, in the 2nd millennium B.C., in Middle America. Sometimes an innovation created by one culture spread to others – like the alphabet. In c.1200 B.C., the Phoenicians were inspired by knowledge of Egyptian hieroglyphics ('picture writing') to create a simplified phonetic script for themselves. A few centuries later, the Greeks adapted this script to write their own language. Later still, the Romans modified it further. The Roman alphabet spread through Europe, and it is the one we use today (although their system of numbering has been replaced for most purposes by the simpler Arabic numerals).

Our knowledge of the ancient world now comes from many sources. Such mighty works as the megalithic stone circles, the Great Wall of China, the pyramids of the Old and New worlds, major irrigation works, have left visible relics. The ruins of ancient settlements are excavated and examined,

with techniques much advanced since the days when 19th-century enthusiasts often tore their way into buried cities and gravemounds with all the subtlety of a terrier at a rat hole. To the modern archaeologist, no detail is too small to be ignored. Middens (rubbish dumps) are as informative as throne-rooms or temples: what people threw away – broken pots and tools, food remains – gives us vivid glimpses into daily life. Tombs tell us a great deal about building skills; and the common practice of providing 'grave goods' for the use of the dead in an afterlife not only demonstrates religious belief but shows what objects were valued by the living. In some cultures the dead took their wealth with them into the next world – the treasure of Egyptian pharoah Tutankhamun is famous today. Less dramatic, but just as revealing, are everyday grave goods: offerings of food, clothing, tools, and household objects.

Standing stones were erected across Europe (this one is in Corsica), suggesting that a single European culture existed to some extent in the Stone Age.

The Parthenon temple (447-438 B.C.) was the largest and most costly building of classical Greece. Its still impressive ruins have made it a model for later architects and earned it the title of the world's most nearly perfect building.

The dead themselves – skeletons, mummies, or 'bog bodies' naturally preserved in acidic bogwater – can speak to us. Bones alone can be scrutinized to reveal an individual's age, sex, height, and general appearance, his state of health and quality of nutrition, even whether he or she was left- or right-handed. Preserved bodies are even more informative. Perhaps the most exhaustive analysis to date was carried out on an Iron Age body found in northwest England in 1984 and known as 'Lindow Man' (the press named him 'Pete Marsh' in honor of the peat bog which preserved his corpse). From scientific examination, we know, for example, that Lindow Man trimmed his hair and beard with scissors, manicured his nails, and suffered mild stomachache caused by worm infestation. We are equally well informed about his death: two head wounds from a narrow-bladed weapon knocked him out before a garotte strangled him and broke his neck – and finally his throat was cut. Such 'overkill' suggests either ritual sacrifice or the execution of a criminal.

In later periods, from c.3500 B.C., archeological evidence is supplemented by contemporary writings, and ancient societies begin to tell us about themselves in their own words. Until recently, only Greek and Roman writings were accessible, but scholarly detective work has now unlocked the secrets of many earlier scripts: laws and histories, store-room records, bills and receipts, sacred writings, public announcements, epic poems, personal letters. One of the most impressive examples is the law code of Hammurabi of Babylon, written in cuneiform script in c.1750 B.C. to record laws made 'so that the strong may not oppress the weak, and to protect the rights of the orphan and widow.' Such writings provide not only factual information but insights into how societies saw themselves (always remembering that written records may treat of how people felt things should be, rather than how they actually were). Sometimes writing preserves traditions of much earlier times, handed down orally for generations: the Greek epic poems, the *Iliad* and *Odyssey*, written down after the 8th century B.C., record the world of the Mycenaeans, four or five centuries earlier. Before the invention of writing, history deals with nations and

Grave goods on a grand scale: in 210 B.C. Emperor Shih Huang-ti of China was buried with 7,500 lifesize models of his soldiers and their mounts.

tribes; but once it became possible to record names, we become aware of individual men and women.

Technological advances in archaeology have made much more information available. Until some 40 years ago, the only accurate dating was derived from the historical records of literate societies. Today the development of radio-carbon dating and dendrochronology (tree-ring dating) has enabled researchers to establish a reliable chronology of world cultures. The surroundings in which people lived are revealed by techniques such as pollen analysis, using pollen samples from the soil of archaeological sites, from artifacts such as mud bricks, or even from the guts of preserved bodies, to tell us what plants grew in a given place and time. Chemical analysis of plant residues shows what people ate: we know from organic matter on cooking pots that people in Peru as early as 200 B.C. regularly ate boiled mashed potatoes; analysis of latrine deposits at a Roman fort in Scotland proved that the legionaries held off the northern barbarians on a diet based largely on bread, with little meat. It is even possible to tell how food was cooked: Lindow Man's last meal was a baked griddle cake, cooked for about half an hour on a flat, heated surface at a low temperature. No detail is too tiny to be informative. Beetle remains in New Stone Age deposits revealed that the recent outbreak of Dutch elm disease in Europe had a counterpart in England some 5000 years ago.

Some archeological evidence takes the form of buried treasure. This ornate dish is part of the Mildenhall Treasure, a hoard of Roman household silver buried in Suffolk, England, in the 4th century A.D.

Models like this show details of costume and equipment that would have disappeared from actual human and animal sacrifices.

In this book (and in its companion volume on the Biblical world), we have tried to open windows on the ancient world for the general reader. Our coverage is, inevitably in so limited a space, largely confined to what we judge to be 'turning points' in human affairs: great social innovations, migrations of peoples, the rise and fall of civilizations, the political developments in Greece and Rome that helped shape western civiliization. But we have also tried to say something about the ordinary people of ancient times, and to show how much like us they were in many ways. We hope that this book will serve as an introduction to the ancient world, as a reminder of how much there is to be learned from it, and as an intimation of how very much more there is to be learned about it. From that old world there is, to borrow the words of the Roman writer Pliny the Elder, 'semper aliquid nova' – always something new.

The family of man

The Australopithecines walked the earth some four million years ago. They were 'near men,' who stood and walked upright and in some ways were more man-like than ape-like, but with relatively small brains and the massive jaws and forward-projecting faces of apes. They had begun to make simple stone tools and to hunt animals for food. Whether the first true early men (*Homo*) descend directly from Australopithecus or merely share a common ancestor is disputed, as is the identification of the earliest *Homo* specimens. Some fossils found at Olduvai Gorge, Tanzania, along with early stone tools, have been named *Homo habilis*, 'handy man,' but the first generally accepted true human was *Homo erectus*, 'upright man,' who lived from 1.5 million years ago. He had mastered the use of fire for warmth, for protection from predators, and possibly for cooking. Later fossils show a gradual change from *Homo erectus* to *Homo sapiens*, modern man. Best known of the early *Homo sapiens* is Neanderthal Man, who lived in Ice Age Europe, from about 70,000 to 35,000 years ago. He hunted large animals like woolly rhinoceros and cave bears with stone clubs and fire-hardened spears. Powerfully built and with heavy brow ridges, he had a large brain and had evidently developed religious beliefs, for he buried his dead with ceremony. He was succeeded by Cro-Magnon Man from southwest Asia, a race very similar in appearance to modern man.

In 1924 this fossil skull was given the name of *Australopithecus africanus* ('southern-ape of Africa') – the first identified 'near man".

Braincase size resembles that of the great apes; the sloping forehead and heavy brows are also ape-like in form.

'Near men' developed man-like jaws long before they developed larger braincases. The jaws are still heavy, but the palate shape, and size, shape, and arrangement of the teeth are markedly more human than ape-like.

Tools like this stone ax provide evidence of the first steps from an animal lifestyle towards the development of a human culture.

Hand-axes, made by chipping flakes off a flint to form a cutting edge, date back to Australopithecus and successor *Homo erectus*.

Compare the shape and scale of a modern foot and the Laetoli footprints.

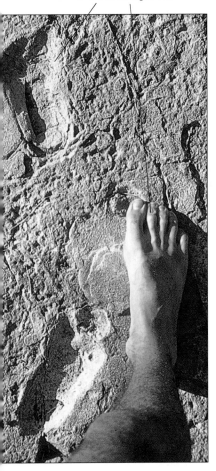

Hominid tracks, preserved in volcanic ash at Laetoli, Tanzania.

The tracks show that the 'near men' walked upright on two legs – leaving the forelimbs free to become arms, with creative hands.

The footprints are those of a hominid family – two adults and a child – who walked across the savanna some 3,750,000 years ago.

FACT FILE

❑ Remains of early hominids (men and near-men) are tantalizingly incomplete and hard to interpret: even dating is often problematic. Even so, these fragments yield much information. A piece of limb bone or pelvis may indicate whether its owner walked upright like modern man; a tooth may place the fossil in the line of human rather than ape ancestry.

❑ The disappearance of Neanderthal Man about 35,000 years ago remains a mystery. Suggested reasons include inability to cope with climatic changes, and deliberate extermination by his successor, Cro-Magnon Man. It is possible that Cro-Magnon Man brought with him diseases for which Neanderthals had no immunity.

❑ The brain of Neanderthal Man was physically larger than that of many modern men.

❑ Biologists studying human genetic material theorize that all modern humans descend from one woman – naturally nicknamed 'Eve' – who lived in Africa c.200,000 years ago.

❑ When bones of Neanderthal Man were discovered in 1857 in the Neander Valley, Germany, not all scientists agreed they were 'the most ancient memorial of the early inhabitants of Europe.' Some said they were the remains of a recently dead Cossack soldier with advanced rickets!

Stone Age art and industry

The first men lived by hunting and by gathering plants; farming was probably not invented until 8000-7000 B.C.. We talk of 'cavemen,' but Neanderthal Man had learned to make tents of animal skins. Cro-Magnon Man improved on his predecessors' tools with a range of spears, arrows, harpoons, and fishing tackle. He also discovered art: painting, engraving, and sculpture. His paintings have survived in caves, where they were protected from the weather. Some 125 caves with prehistoric artwork have been discovered in Europe, the oldest dating from at least 30,000 B.C. Lively, lifelike portrayals of animals are frequent, and were perhaps meant to give hunters magical powers over their prey. Paintings of pregnant animals may symbolize the fertility of the herds upon which the hunters depended. Human figures also appear, hunting, dancing, or performing mysterious rituals. Small, stylized figures of heavily pregnant women, known as 'Venuses,' may be the oldest representations of a fertility goddess. After Cro-Magnon Man, the inventions of later races came thick and fast. Hunting and gathering food gave way to sowing crops and raising livestock; men dug deep flint-mines, sewed clothes with bone needles, and paddled wooden boats. By the Neolithic, or New Stone Age, people living in small villages connected by roads had developed both industry, with axe and pottery 'factories,' and trade, and had some knowledge of math and astronomy.

This dramatic bison was painted c.19,000 years ago at Altamira, Spain. Food animals, including mammoth, boar, and reindeer, are the dominant theme of the cave artist.

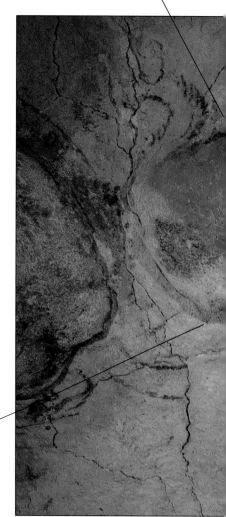

Stone Age 'Venuses,' like this example from Willendorf, Austria, make the female form a symbol of maternity. The whole focus is on the pregnant torso, with a knob for the head, no face, and simplified limbs.

The function of cave art was probably magical rather than simply decorative, reflecting the importance of animals for food and skins. By painting this bison, the painter may have hoped to gain power over the living animal.

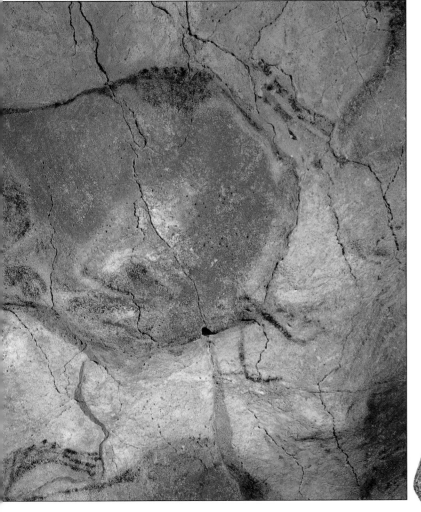

❏ A Stone Age sculptor's 'workshop' was found at Dolní Věstonice, Czechoslovakia. Many small clay animals in various stages of completion were scattered around a large hearth.

❏ Cave artists made their 'paints' from mineral pigments such as ochers, producing a range of reds, blacks, browns, and yellows. When the first cave paintings were discovered in 1940 at Altamira, Spain, few people were willing to believe that primitive man could have produced them, and their finder was accused of forgery.

❏ The Neolithic village of Skara Brae (below) in Orkney, Scotland, was preserved when it was buried by a sandstorm nearly 3,000 years ago. Its stone houses have fireplaces and built-in stone furniture, including box beds, shelves, and closets. There is even a drainage sewer, complete with inspection chambers.

This bison from the cave of Niaux, France, bears two arrows. Paintings of wounded animals may be meant as hunting magic, to aid the hunter.

Flint ax head, 3000 B.C. The maker shaped his ax by chipping flakes off, using bone or stone. Finally he produced a sharp cutting edge by grinding it smooth with wet sand.

Rings of stone

These imposing trilithons (two upright stones supporting a horizontal one) form part of Britain's most famous circle, Stonehenge. Building work began at Stonehenge c.2800 B.C. and continued for more than 1,000 years, during which the plan was modified four times. The ring's axis is aligned to sunrise on Midsummer Day (June 24).

The bones of Stone Age people in western Europe tell a story of short, hard lives. Signs of malnutrition and severe arthritis are common. The majority of children died in infancy, and very few people lived into their thirties. These subsistence farmers lived in log houses, made simple pots of local clay, and shaped tools from stone and antler. But they also built towering stone edifices which show considerable engineering and artistic skills. Notable are the stone circles of Britain and France, erected over a period of some 2,000 years from the New Stone Age (c.3300 B.C.) to the Late Bronze Age (c.1200 B.C.). Nearly 1,000 survive in Britain alone, from small 'family-size' rings of boulders to the great circles of Stonehenge and Avebury. The Avebury Ring, Britain's largest, measures 440yd (402m) across, and originally comprised some 600 stones, of which only 76 survive today. The urge that drove men to haul and raise monoliths weighing up to 50 tons must have been powerful: it is most likely that the stone circles had religious significance. Many stones are aligned with the sun or moon, so some have speculated that the rings served as giant, primitive computers to predict eclipses and solstices. Certainly the makers of the circles had a knowledge of astronomy, as well as an understanding of the mechanics involved in moving great weights by manpower alone.

The burial chamber of Newgrange, Ireland (c.2500 B.C.) is edged by 97 large slabs and covered by a cairn of smaller stones.

Mysterious carved spirals and lozenges appear on many of Britain's Stone Age monuments.

Mnajdra Temple, a rock temple of a type unique to Malta, dates from c.2800 B.C. Its upright slabs and capstones recall Stonehenge.

The tops of the upright stones were cut back to leave pegs, which slot into holes cut on the underside of the lintel stones.

Lintel stones lying perfectly horizontal across the uprights bear witness to the builders' skill.

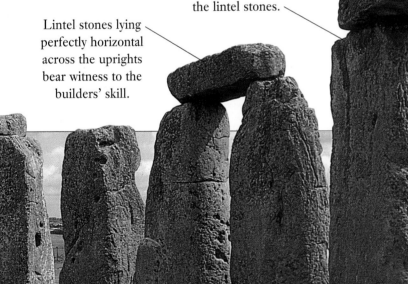

❏ Stone Age circles were sometimes built with wooden posts, not stones. At Woodhenge (Wiltshire, England), concentric ovals of postholes show where a timber circle was built in c.2300 B.C. At nearby Stonehenge, it is apparent that the stones were shaped and fitted together by men skilled in building in wood, using pegs and dowels and mortise-and-tenon joints.

❏ At many circles, archaeologists have found evidence of ritual offerings: fragments of burnt human bone and deliberately broken pottery.

❏ The 40 bluestones of Stonehenge came originally from southwest Wales, nearly 160mi (257km) away. Researchers have long marveled how prehistoric men transported these 4 ton monoliths. Recent research suggests the stones perhaps were carried to the Salisbury Plain area by the movement of glaciers during the Ice Age.

❏ Stone Age man began to practice medicine – even advanced surgery. Some skulls show evidence of trephination, an operation to cut out a disk of bone. Healed bone round the operation site shows that some patients at least survived the treatment. Trephination is still used by surgeons treating skull fractures or tumors – and by primitive peoples to release devils, believed to cause headaches or insanity.

Funeral rites

Neanderthal burials, with grave offerings of food and tools, offer the first evidence of belief in an afterlife. Later societies developed ever more elaborate funeral rituals. As early as 5700 B.C., skilled Neolithic architects built chambered tombs for communal burials. These 'houses of the dead' are hewn from solid rock or, more often, built of massive boulders known as megaliths ('big stones'), and covered with high mounds of earth. They must have needed the cooperative labor of whole tribes. Complex funeral rites included decomposition of bodies in vast mortuary enclosures before the bones were laid in their tombs. In early Bronze Age Europe, cremation became the fashion, and ashes were buried in large urns. The dead were provided with goods, often deliberately broken (i.e., themselves 'dead'), for use in the afterlife, and human sacrifice seems to have accompanied some burials. In the same period, Ancient Egyptians mummified their dead to preserve the appearance of life, housing them in the first stone pyramids, with lavish grave goods. The objects buried with the dead give us vivid insights into ancient civilizations. Tools, weapons, and jewelry often survive; more rarely, perishable objects such as clothes and furniture. Sometimes we encounter the dead themselves, from artifically preserved Egyptian mummies to European Iron Age people naturally 'tanned' in peat bogs.

The Step Pyramid of King Zoser (c.2620 B.C.) was Egypt's first major stone building, based on earlier brickwork structures.

❑ A common form of megalithic tomb is the dolmen, a chamber created by upright stones roofed over by a horizontal capstone, often of great size. The largest capstone on record is that of the Browneshill Dolmen, County Carlow, Ireland, estimated to weigh 100 tons.

❑ The severe climate of Siberia caused 'deep-freezing' of Scythian grave-mounds of c.600-400 B.C. This preserved the embalmed bodies as well as a wealth of fragile grave goods, such as woven shirts, carpets, and decorative felt-work.

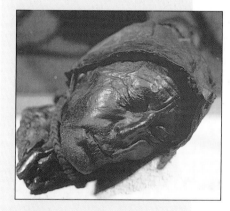

The dolmen of Rondossec (Brittany, France). Dolmens, or chambered tombs, were communal vaults, opened for successive burials over many years. The great slabs were originally covered by a mound of earth or stones

The popular spiral motif carved in stone at Newgrange burial chamber (page 20) is here incised in clay.

Bronze Age cremation urn (France). Such urns were buried in existing mounds or in new cemeteries – 'urnfields.' Some urn burials seem to have been accompanied by child sacrifices.

Royal tombs had to be protected from grave robbers. The Step Pyramid looks forbidding enough; but the actual burial chamber is hidden far below, down an 88ft (27m) shaft and beyond a complex network of underground galleries.

❑ Danish peat bogs have yielded a number of Iron Age bodies, some so well preserved that they were taken for modern murder victims. Analysis of the stomach contents of a man found at Tollund Fen (above) made it possible to reconstruct the meal he ate 2,000 years ago: a thin porridge of cultivated grains and weed seeds. In 1954 archeologists recreated this recipe and sampled it. It was not to their liking!

23

Matters of record

Terracotta tablet, 3000 B.C., from Uruk, bearing the picture-symbols which were to evolve into the earliest writing. Symbols etched on clay tablets followed the use, from 8000 B.C., of shaped clay tokens to record merchants' stock.

The peoples of the ancient world developed writing to record trading deals. It soon became not merely a useful tool, but a source of knowledge and power. The oldest known script is that of the Uruk culture of Mesopotamia (in modern Iraq) and dates to c.3500 B.C. It began with small sketches of trade objects, which evolved first into symbols and then into a wedge-shaped script (cuneiform), easy to cut in wet clay with a sharp reed. This useful skill gradually spread to other kingdoms, although not all used cuneiform. The Indus civilization of South Asia (c.2500-1500 B.C.) used a pictographic script, again chiefly for trade purposes. The Egyptians probably got the idea of writing from Asia, but from c.3000 B.C. created their own complex pictographic scripts. A little before 1000 B.C., the Phoenicians invented a standardized alphabet of 22 characters (all consonants) to keep business records. Greek traders adopted this, adding vowels. Later still, the Romans developed the alphabet, loosely based on the Greek version, that we use in the West today. Other forms of writing were independently invented elsewhere. In China, a pictographic ('picture writing') script was created during the Shang Dynasty (1523-1027 B.C.), and was used on 'oracle bones' for divination purposes. In the New World, the Maya created their own pictographs, bearing no resemblance to any other known script, to record astronomical lore and royal dynasties.

One of the earliest uses of writing was to make name-tags and trade-marks, identifying the owner of goods and property. The inscription on this cylinder seal of c.2000 B.C. enabled its owner to stamp his name, 'Lambazi, son of Atu, Brewer,' on his goods. Such seals are often works of art.

❏ The wellknown hieroglyphics are only one of three scripts developed by ancient Egyptians. Hieroglyphs were the earliest, and remained the official script used for inscriptions; later, simplified forms, called hieratic and demotic, were introduced for less formal use.

❏ The Shang Dynasty script of Bronze Age China can claim to be the oldest form of writing still in use. A standardized form introduced by the Ch'in Dynasty in 221 B.C. is still used today.

❏ Shang Dynasty writing is preserved on 'oracle bones', used to seek guidance. A question was inscribed on a bone, and it was heated until cracks appeared. The answer was 'read' in the shape of these cracks – and sometimes recorded in writing on the bone. Shang rulers consulted the oracle bones before taking any action, and in consequence many inscriptions record the deeds of kings and their battles.

❏ A tiny fragment of bone bearing more than 1,000 marks was identified in 1991 as the earliest European calendar. It was found in a cave in southwest France and is believed to be some 12,000 years old.

❏ The pictographs of the Maya of Mesoamerica are unlike any other known script, and were not deciphered until the 1960s.

A version of the cuneiform script was still in use as late as the first century A.D. This example is a Babylonian syllabary (a scribe's reference table of syllables) from 442 B.C.

Egyptian stela (stone column) of 600 B.C., recording in hieroglyphs, 'The eye of Horus is against them.' Horus, the falcon god, is shown center right.

Classical Egyptian hieroglyphics comprise some 700 symbols, based on human figures, parts of the human body, birds, animals, plants, tools, or furnishings.

Each symbol of this complex script could have several meanings, representing a sound or an idea, or relating to neighboring signs.

Battles long ago

The earliest surviving wooden implement, dating back c.200,000 years, is a spear head of yew wood. Perhaps its maker intended it for hunting – but he would also have used it (along with a stone ax, or perhaps a long bow with flint-tipped arrows) against anyone who infringed on his hunting grounds. We cannot precisely date the first 'war' between sizable communities; but we know that as early as c.7000 B.C. the people of Jericho in the Jordan Valley protected their settlement against invasion with walls and a moat. By c.3500 B.C. the Mesopotamian state of Sumer was defended by citizen soldiers armed with metal-tipped spears (for thrusting, not throwing) and protected by bronze helmets and leather shields. They were sufficiently disciplined to maneuver in large formations (phalanxes; c.60-80 strong), directed by officers riding in four-wheeled carts drawn by asses. By c.2000 B.C. Mesopotamian armies had 'strike forces' of war chariots. These played a key role in the war in which Egypt drove out its Hyksos overlords in c.1540 B.C. The two-horse, two-wheeled chariot carried a driver and a fighter, the latter armed with javelins and a bow. They were often used in great numbers: the Hittites are recorded to have deployed 3, 500 chariots against the Egyptians at the battle of Kadesh in 1286 B.C. A major infantry weapon at this time was the mace – either a short, heavy 'skull cracker' or a lighter, long-handled 'pole axe'; foot soldiers also carried spears, slings, and bows. The sword, although used since very early times, did not become a standard infantry weapon until its adoption by the Assyrians after c.1200 B.C.

Packed shoulder to shoulder, with shields forming a protective wall, Sumerian spearmen advance in the mass formation called a phalanx.

Close fitting helmets protect the warriors from missiles. This stone tablet was made to mark a Sumerian victory in 3000-2500 B.C.

A sword of the later Bronze Age looks impressive; but bronze swords had little durability and were of limited use in battle.

Tools designed for hunting – like this harpoon head of bone, carved in Western Europe before c.10,000 B.C. – became weapons in humanity's earliest fights.

War prisoners are marched through the streets of Nineveh: a carving from the palace of Ashurbanipal (669-626 B.C.), who was one of Assyria's greatest warrior kings.

'Antenna' hilted bronze sword is more status symbol than weapon.

With its vicious barbs, this bone harpoon would have inflicted dreadful wounds on beast or man. It is the ancestor of the spear, major weapon of most ancient armies.

Assyrian dignitaries ride in a wagon drawn by oxen. Heavy chariots, drawn by two horses and carrying a driver and up to three archers or spearmen, and iron weapons, made Assyria a much feared nation.

FACT FILE

❑ The Assyrians were masters of war in c.1200-600 B.C., their battlefield tactics skilfully blending the operations of well armored infantrymen (above) with straight bladed iron swords; heavy chariots carrying up to four archers or spearmen; and horse archers and slingers. (True cavalry, armed with thrusting weapons, did not become of great importance until the development of the stirrup after c.A.D. 500.)

❑ The composite bow, perhaps developed by the Akkadians after c.2300 B.C., had a deeply curved stave made of wood, horn, and animal sinew, glued together in layers. It was far more powerful than the long bow known since Neolithic times. A skilled archer might hit targets at up to 250yd (230m) while firing from a chariot at full gallop.

❑ Sailing ships and oared galleys appeared in the Mediterranean by c.3000 B.C. The first naval battle on record was in c.2700 B.C., when ships sent raiding by Pharaoh Zoser of Egypt clashed with Phoenician vessels.

Images of the world

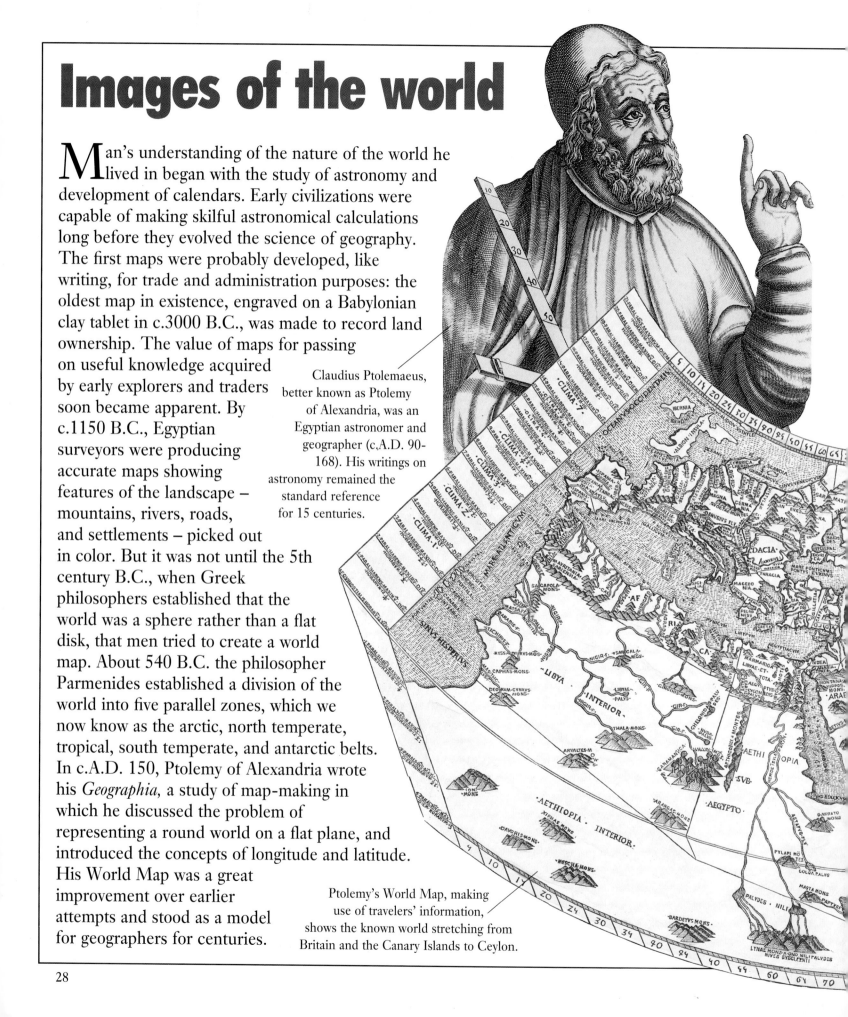

Man's understanding of the nature of the world he lived in began with the study of astronomy and development of calendars. Early civilizations were capable of making skilful astronomical calculations long before they evolved the science of geography. The first maps were probably developed, like writing, for trade and administration purposes: the oldest map in existence, engraved on a Babylonian clay tablet in c.3000 B.C., was made to record land ownership. The value of maps for passing on useful knowledge acquired by early explorers and traders soon became apparent. By c.1150 B.C., Egyptian surveyors were producing accurate maps showing features of the landscape – mountains, rivers, roads, and settlements – picked out in color. But it was not until the 5th century B.C., when Greek philosophers established that the world was a sphere rather than a flat disk, that men tried to create a world map. About 540 B.C. the philosopher Parmenides established a division of the world into five parallel zones, which we now know as the arctic, north temperate, tropical, south temperate, and antarctic belts. In c.A.D. 150, Ptolemy of Alexandria wrote his *Geographia,* a study of map-making in which he discussed the problem of representing a round world on a flat plane, and introduced the concepts of longitude and latitude. His World Map was a great improvement over earlier attempts and stood as a model for geographers for centuries.

Claudius Ptolemaeus, better known as Ptolemy of Alexandria, was an Egyptian astronomer and geographer (c.A.D. 90-168). His writings on astronomy remained the standard reference for 15 centuries.

Ptolemy's World Map, making use of travelers' information, shows the known world stretching from Britain and the Canary Islands to Ceylon.

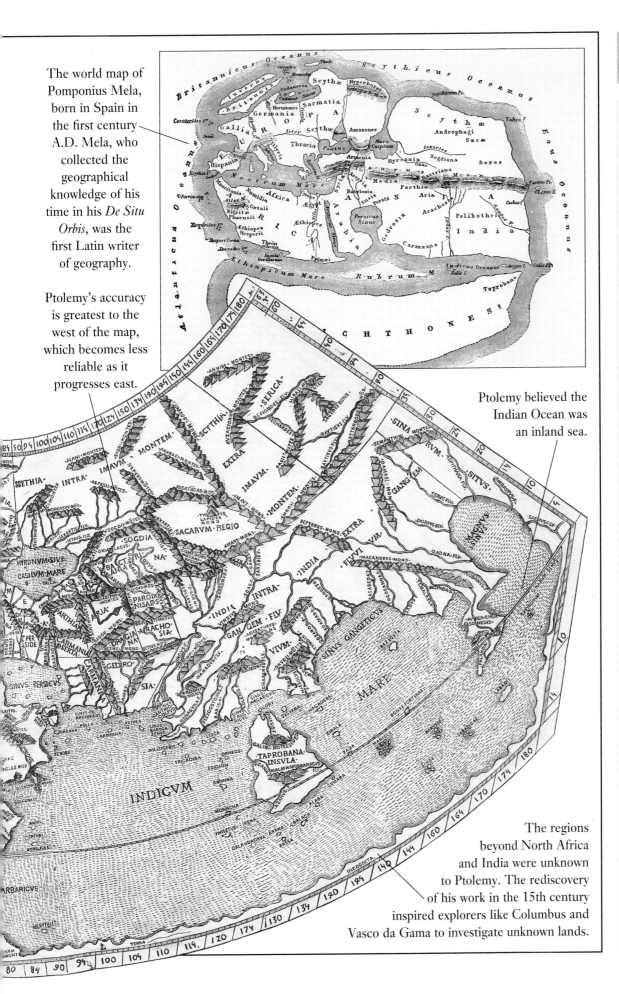

The world map of Pomponius Mela, born in Spain in the first century A.D. Mela, who collected the geographical knowledge of his time in his *De Situ Orbis*, was the first Latin writer of geography.

Ptolemy's accuracy is greatest to the west of the map, which becomes less reliable as it progresses east.

Ptolemy believed the Indian Ocean was an inland sea.

The regions beyond North Africa and India were unknown to Ptolemy. The rediscovery of his work in the 15th century inspired explorers like Columbus and Vasco da Gama to investigate unknown lands.

❑ Greek philosophers may have derived their discovery that the world was a sphere from the experience of sailors navigating by the stars. Master mariners had long known that the sky's appearance changed as they steered north or south, and that shapes appearing on the horizon disappeared over a curve rather than a flat line. By 500 B.C. teachers like Pythagoras had established the concept of a spherical world – a knowledge that was later to be lost, and re-established centuries later.

❑ In the 3rd century B.C., Eratosthenes, a librarian at Alexandria, made an accurate calculation of the earth's polar circumference (c.25,000mi/12,700km).

❑ From c.600 B.C. the Greek city of Miletus (in modern Turkey) became a center of geographical knowledge. There, in 550 B.C., Anaximander (below) created a new kind of map, showing the world as viewed from above, and 50 years later Hecateus produced the first geography book.

The first Americans

Part of a gorget (ornament worn at the throat) elaborately carved in shell, found in a burial mound at Craig, Oklahoma.

Spear point, c.8000 B.C., from Agate Basin, Wyoming. Razor-sharp stone points produced effective hunting spears: Stone Age kill sites reveal the bones of whole herds of animals with spear points in them.

The story of man in the Americas began long after his appearance in the Old World. No fossils of humans before *Homo sapiens* have been found in the New World, and archaeologists believe that men arrived in North America only 40,000 years ago. Then, a land bridge across the Bering Strait linked America with Asia, enabling Ice Age hunters from Siberia to cross to Alaska. Today, a physical resemblance between Amerindian and northeast Asian peoples attests to common ancestry. America was good country for hunters with stone weapons, and many tribes followed the hunter-gatherer lifestyle until the coming of the Europeans, although some were practicing agriculture by c.1000 B.C. They knew the arts of weaving and pottery, produced fine craftwork, and developed complex funeral rites. The Adena culture of Ohio (c.1000 B.C.-A.D. 200) was the first of the famous Mound Builders, making vast earthworks: burial mounds and huge earthen 'sculptures' in animal or geometric forms. Their successors, the highly advanced Hopewell Indians (c.300 B.C.-c.A.D. 400) built even larger mounds and created exquisite artifacts in exotic materials such as copper, sheet mica, obsidian, and soapstone. The scale of their communal grave mounds (up to 40ft/12m high) evidences a highly organized society, as does their wide trading network, bringing raw materials from regions as widely separated as Florida and the Rocky Mountains.

Shells, feathers, or porcupine quills were utilized to make jewelry. Large shells provided material for carving, as here; others were ground into colored beads.

Cliff Palace ruins at Mesa Verde, Colorado. The Amasazi culture (c.100 B.C.-A.D. 1300) began with underground houses, then moved aboveground, and from A.D. 1000 built cliff dwellings.

FACT FILE

❏ Mound building continued until A.D. 1500. The Mississippian culture, perhaps influenced by contact with civilizations south of Mexico like the Aztecs, built giant flat-topped mounds crowned by temples. A famous example is Monk's Mound, Illinois (below) (A.D. 900-1150): 100ft (30.5m) high and covering 16 acres (6.5ha).

❏ The modern Aleuts and Inuit of Alaska are more closely related to Siberian people than to other Native American tribes. Their ancestors came to America later than other tribes (c. 3000-1000 B.C.), crossing the Bering Sea by boat and not by the Bering Strait land bridge.

❏ American cultures did not develop the bow and arrow until c.1000 B.C. Some 6,000 years earlier, the Folsom culture of New Mexico had invented the *atlatl*, a catapult device of wood and leather which enabled a hunter to throw his spear harder and farther than by hand.

❏ Dried cobs of cultivated corn found in Bat Cave, New Mexico, and dating to c.3500 B.C. provide the first evidence of farming north of Mexico.

Adena Indians built the Great Serpent Mound, Ohio, in the form of a snake, 1,330ft (40.5m) long – probably as a shrine honoring the clan's totem, or emblem.

Built against the canyon wall, the 'Cliff Palace' is no palace but a village. Large apartment blocks combine dwellings and storehouses.

After 1300, the great cliff settlements were abandoned. War, crop-destroying drought, or timber depletion may have been causes of the move.

31

A place in the sun

The earliest great Mesoamerican (Middle American) civilization was the Olmec culture of Mexico, which emerged c.1200 B.C. The Olmecs were farmers who developed a highly organized society with a rigid social and religious class structure. They built great ceremonial centers, with pyramid temples, and maintained them over centuries with a vast labor force. Their highly skilled stone-carvers worked in hard materials such as jadeite, imported from considerable distances. They created huge sculptured heads, carved from imported basalt and serpentine and often up to 12ft (3.7m) high. 'Baby-faced' jaguar figurines are also common, suggesting a major religious cult centering on this beast. The Olmec civilization came to an end c.600-400 B.C., when its main centers were destroyed or abandoned, but it helped shape subsequent cultures. The Zapotecs, the Olmecs' successors after c.500 B.C., built the great city of Monte Alban on the west coast of Mexico. Here were found the first evidences of New World hieroglyphic writing, a system of calculation, and calendrical knowledge based on study of the stars. Farther south, in Peru, in c.1000-200 B.C., the Chavin culture dominated the Andes. Great builders, the Chavin take their name from their magnificent temple at Chavin de Huantar. Their distinctive art style mingles stylized figures of men, jaguars, serpents, and eagles in intricate flowing patterns. The Chavin made several technological advances, including an improved strain of maize, a new type of loom, and metal-working skills.

Olmec head in jadeite. From 1500 B.C. Olmec craftsmen worked this rare stone: too hard to carve, it was ground with natural abrasives such as wet sand.

The Moon Pyramid, one of two great pyramids at Teotihuacan, from c.100 B.C. Mesoamerica's first major city. By A.D. 150 it covered 8sq mi (20sq km).

The pyramid was built of earth and rubble, covered with dressed stone blocks. All was carried by manpower: Mesoamerica never developed wheeled transport.

Wall painting from a tomb in the city of Monte Alban. The bright colors of the elaborate ritual costumes shown here were achieved by master dyers, who manufactured a wide range of pigments from bugs, plants, and even shell-fish.

The stepped surface bears no decoration, and is broken only by stairs which led to a shrine on top.

❏ Built as a ceremonial center in honor of the jaguar god Cosijo, Monte Alban (above) was the Zapotec capital for more than 500 years. Buildings were set on vast stone platforms, honeycombed with galleries and surrounded by pyramids and grand staircases. When the Zapotec empire fell, the city was abandoned, to be sacked by the neighboring state of Mixtec.

❏ Jaguar worship was common to many Mesoamerican civilizations. The Olmecs reshaped their own skulls in imitation of the jaguar's, binding children's heads while the bones were still soft to achieve the desired flattened shape.

❏ Despite the occupation of most of their territory, from the 14th century A.D., by the rival Mixtecs and Aztecs, the Zapotecs survived as a people, and their language is still spoken today. Benito Juárez, president of Mexico (1806-72), was a full-blooded Zapotec.

The vanished empire

While the Olmecs dominated Mexico, the rainforests of Guatemala and Yucatan saw the dawn of the Maya civilization – a culture dedicated to the measurement of time. From simple villagers living in forest clearings and building small temples, the Maya had developed by c.A.D. 300 into a highly advanced yet ritual-bound people. They built several hundred ceremonial centers, with lofty, stepped pyramid temples, palaces, and markets, all adorned with sculptures and carved pillars. Despite these magnificent works of architecture, Mayan building techniques remained those of the Stone Age. At the same time, their religious beliefs led them to develop a sophisticated arithmetic, a complex script, astronomical knowledge, and a calendar unrivaled for centuries. Accurate timing of rituals was essential to the Maya, and their 'Long Count' calendar calculated not only the days of the year, but vast cycles of years within an infinity of time. Its precision was so great that Mayan computation of the solar year differs from modern reckoning by a mere eight-thousandth of a day. For some 600 years this prosperous culture lived by its elaborate calendrical system. But during the 9th century Mayan civilization collapsed. Archaeological discoveries made in 1991 at Dos Pilas (near Antigua city, Guatemala) suggest that around A.D. 800 a Mayan ruler launched a civil war so fierce that no crops could be raised. Mayan society depended on a small, elite priesthood concentrated in a few major centers: faced with starvation, these collapsed and the whole society toppled with them.

The stirrup-shaped spout and painted scene portraying a demon are typical of the pottery jars of the Mochica culture of Peru (c.A.D. 50-800).

The Maya ceremonial centre of Chichen Itza, Mexico, was founded c.A.D. 900, although this huge step pyramid was built after 1194. Known as the Castillo, it honors the Plumed Serpent deity.

The Temple of the Warriors, Chichen Itza. The vast stone temple crowning the step pyramid still contains its stone altar mounted upon 19 carved figures.

The Court of the Thousand Columns, adjoining the Temple of the Warriors, was found in 1842 by U.S. traveler John Lloyd Stephens.

❏ The Mayan mathematical system was the first to contain a symbol for zero. It enabled the Maya to carry out complex calculations involving very large numbers – a need perhaps arising from the smallness and cheapness of their money unit, the cocoa bean.

❏ Toys with wheels prove that the Maya knew the wheel; yet they made no practical use of their knowledge for vehicles.

❏ The Mayan script has more than 800 hieroglyphs, many of which remain untranslated – although the Mayan calendar was decoded in 1880.

❏ Mayan ceremonial centers included a court for ball games, much like the modern football stadium, complete with stands for spectators in their thousands. Teams of players kept a heavy rubber ball in constant motion, aiming to knock it through a ring at the side of the court. They played rough: injuries and even deaths were common.

❏ The gods of the death-obsessed Maya were a terrifying assembly, given to inflicting catastrophes on mankind. They included moon goddess Ixchel, who sent floods to destroy; and Ixtab, goddess of suicide, who is portrayed hanging from a tree, partly decomposed. Even the creator god Hunab was far from kindly, and destroyed the world three times before losing interest in it.

China: the Middle Kingdom

The prosperous peasant culture of Chinese Stone Age farmers, shut off from outside influences by the sea to the east and the Tibetan plateau to the west, led to the early development of a great civilization. The earliest recorded rule is that of the Bronze Age Shang Dynasty (1523-1027 B.C.), which began to draw together the loose confederacy of states under one emperor. This was a feudal society whose emperor, claiming divine descent, was not an absolute ruler but first among equals. The Shang period is notable for superb bronzeworking, sculptures in jade, limestone, and marble, the introduction of silk weaving, and the earliest Chinese script, in the form of oracular writings scratched on 'dragon bones.' In 1027 B.C. the Shang Dynasty was overthrown by the Chou, a group of tribesmen from west China, whose rule lasted 800 years, to 221 B.C. Under the Chou Dynasty the realm was greatly extended. Technological developments included the introduction of iron, the development of irrigation, and the invention of the crossbow. The teachings of the Chou philosopher Confucius (551-479 B.C.) were to have a lasting effect upon Chinese society and political practice. He believed in a harmonious society founded upon dutiful relationships between righteous superiors and obedient inferiors. Confucianism was influential in creating a powerful unified society in China.

High-shouldered wine vessels, with two ring handles near the top and a third lower down, were popular from Shang to Middle Chou times.

Shang Dynasty bronzeworkers cast elaborately decorated vessels like this from clay molds, with the patterns modeled in relief on the inside.

The Chou Dynasty continued the tradition of fine bronzework. This decorative elephant is actually a ritual vessel for wine, with a lid in the animal's back.

The Shang Empire, built around the fertile plains of the Hwang-ho and Yangtse Rivers, was probably less of an empire than a loose confederation of clans. The Shang emperors ruled from a central capital, which was moved six times: two, at Cheng-chou and Anyang, have now been excavated.

Shang Dynasty tripod ritual bronze vase. Tripod water and cooking vessels are characteristic of ancient China.

Bronzesmiths of ancient China were inspired by the animal kingdom. They made animal-shaped vessels like this, or adorned lids and handles with animal heads; stylized decorations are often based on animal forms, especially the tiger and dragon.

Bronze Age China produced more than 20 types of ritual vessels for offerings of food or drink, some based on earlier pottery designs.

The Shang state was one of dramatic class division. While bronzework like this was created for a Bronze Age aristocracy, poor people were still living in the Stone Age.

FACT FILE

❏ The teachings of Confucius (above) have been followed for more than 2,000 years, yet he failed to win recognition during his lifetime. He resigned his ministerial post in the state of Lu when the ruler rejected his advice, and for years traveled from court to court seeking in vain a post where he could practice his theories.

❏ China's first major culture developed along the Hwang-Ho, or Yellow River, where fertile, easily-worked soil provided ideal conditions. Here, peasants of the Stone Age Yang-shao culture established a peaceful agricultural society based on large villages.

❏ The Shang state centered on a large capital city. An early capital at Cheng-chou spread over nearly 9 acres (3.6ha): it had a regular street-plan and walls 23ft (7m) high. About 1300 B.C. the capital moved to Anyang, where elaborate royal tombs contain splendid weapons, jewelry, and chariots, as well as animal and human sacrifices.

Empire behind the Wall

Towards the end of the Chou Dynasty, its power was more apparent than real as its vassal states, notably the Ch'in, strove for control of the kingdom. The Ch'in state had been growing in strength since c.350 B.C., aided by military innovations unknown to its rivals: the use of cavalry instead of war-chariots and the early adoption of iron weapons. The period c.403-256 B.C., when Chou and Ch'in fought for mastery, is called the Age of the Warring States. Shih Huang-ti led the Ch'in to victory in 256 B.C., and became First Emperor of a newly unified China (whose modern name derives from the Ch'in). The Ch'in Dynasty outlived Shih Huang-ti by only four years, but its achievements were impressive. The First Emperor divided China into 36 provinces for purposes of government and established laws and taxes.

This elaborate gadget is the first Chinese seismograph earthquake recorder), invented in c.A.D. 132 by Han Dynasty mathematician and astronomer Chang Heng.

He standardized weights, measures, coinage, systems of writing, and even the axle-width of carts throughout the empire. He also set an army of laborers to build the Great Wall along 2,5000mi (4,020 km) of China's frontier, to keep out nomads from Mongolia. The murder of his successor in 207 B.C. led to the birth of the Han Dynasty, which endured until A.D. 220. The Han made great strides in state administration and public education, as well as in art and technology. Sundials, water clocks, and seismographs to predict and record earthquakes were invented, and for the first time China was opened to outside trade. Under the Ch'in and Han, China's empire of 60 million people became a great state.

Eight gaping toads await an earthquake to dislodge a ball from a dragon's head above. The toad facing the tremor catches the ball.

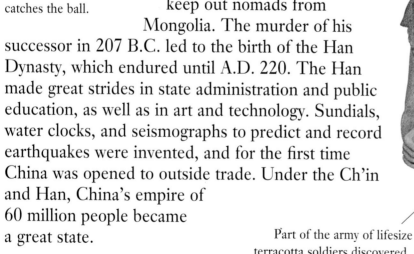

Part of the army of lifesize terracotta soldiers discovered guarding the grave of Emperor Shih Huang-ti when it was opened in the late 1970s.

Section of the Great Wall, near Peking. The Wall was begun in 221 B.C., incorporating small-scale earlier fortifications. Rebuilt many times, the present Wall (half its original length) is a Ming Dynasty (1368-1644 A.D.) restoration.

The faces of the figures are all different, perhaps portraits of the emperor's guards. These figures stood in for the human sacrifices of Shang times – a change of custom which Confucius approved.

When Shih Huang-ti came to power, one of his first acts as emperor was the introduction of conscription to set up a state army. The size of the pottery army gives some concept of the forces at his command.

FACT FILE

❏ It took 700,000 laborers to build the vast tomb of the Ch'in emperor Shih Huang-ti and the man-made mountain over it. Its interior depicts the empire in miniature, with mountains and rivers; the ceiling shows the heavens. The emperor's body was guarded by an army of more than 7,500 lifesize terracotta warriors and their animals.

❏ Until 202 B.C., Liu Pang was a minor official of peasant origins. When the assassination of Shih Huang-ti's successor left the throne vacant, Liu Pang defeated the aristocratic general Hsiang Yu and seized power. As Emperor Kao-tsu, he became the founder of the powerful Han Dynasty.

❏ Shih Huang Ti, China's 'First Emperor,' commemorated his victories by raising a copy of the palace of each rival he defeated. Before his death in 221 B.C. he is said to have built 270 of these palaces.

❏ The tomb of Prince Liu Sheng (died 113 B.C.) and his wife, Tou Wan, was dug 170ft (52m) into a hillside and closed with massive stone doors sealed with molten iron. Opening in 1968 revealed 2,800 grave goods, including 6 carriages and the skeletons of 16 horses. The royal couple had been buried in suits of jade, believed to have magical powers of preservation, but within this casing their bodies had crumbled to dust.

People of the Pacific

The earliest history of the major Pacific islands, Australia and Japan, is that of seafarers. Archaeological evidence suggests that humans did not evolve here, but came by sea from various parts of Asia in migrations beginning up to 60,000 years ago. The original inhabitants of Australia are thought to have come from Southeast Asia, perhaps 40,000 years ago, and largely by land, for a land bridge then joined Borneo and Indochina. Even so, migrants had to cross c.50mi (80km) stretches of sea in primitive canoes – perhaps the first long voyages in human history. Some Australian Aborigines preserved the hunter-gatherer lifestyle of their ancestors into the present century. The first settlers in Japan came by sea from China, Manchuria, and Korea, c.40-50,000 years ago. They may have bequeathed to their descendants an established belief in their racial superiority that led to the founding of a great empire: much Japanese mythology reflects this (although it was not written down until the 8th century A.D.). By 1400 B.C. Japan had begun to develop a farming economy, eventually based upon rice. According to Japanese tradition, the Japanese Empire was founded in 660 B.C. (more probably, it is thought, in c.20 B.C.) by Jimmu Tenno, first emperor, from whom the present Emperor Akihito is 125th in direct line of descent. By the 4th century A.D., imperial rule extended over most of western Japan. Soon, contact with Korea led to the adoption of Chinese script and immigration by Koreans and Manchurians, who brought such technical skills as wood-block printing, and also the Buddhist faith.

The Easter Islanders of the South Pacific, of Polynesian descent, developed a great culture (A.D 1100-1680) whose legacy includes some 600 mysterious giant statues.

Effigy of Kwannon, Buddhist goddess of mercy, in Todai-ji Temple, Japan. Buddhist teaching reached Japan via China and was widely adopted. Its arrival helped to formalize the native Shinto cult; although some fusion of the two religions soon occurred.

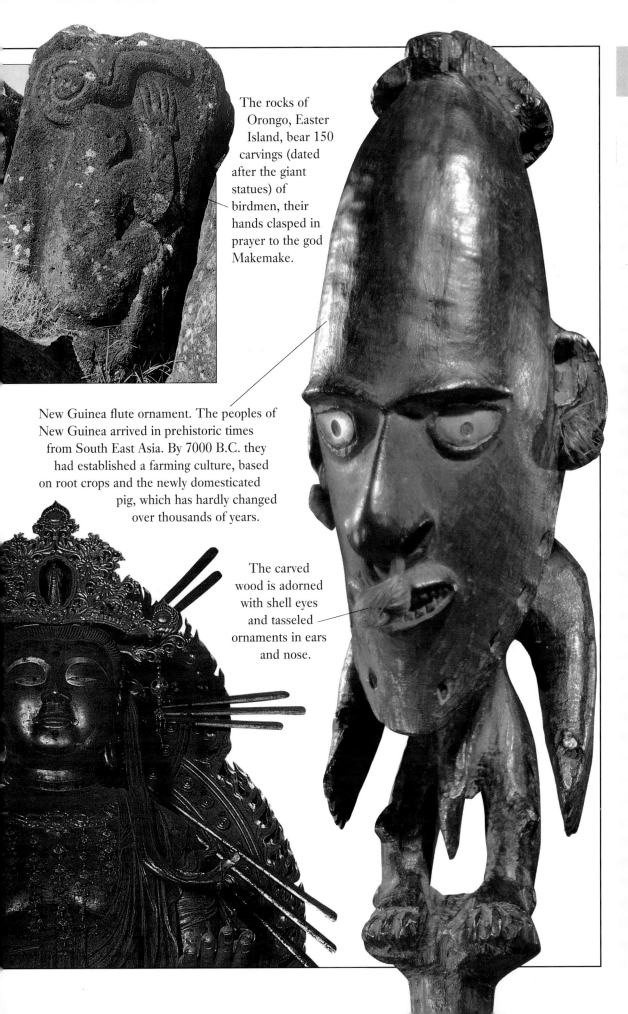

The rocks of Orongo, Easter Island, bear 150 carvings (dated after the giant statues) of birdmen, their hands clasped in prayer to the god Makemake.

New Guinea flute ornament. The peoples of New Guinea arrived in prehistoric times from South East Asia. By 7000 B.C. they had established a farming culture, based on root crops and the newly domesticated pig, which has hardly changed over thousands of years.

The carved wood is adorned with shell eyes and tasseled ornaments in ears and nose.

FACT FILE

❏ Australian fossils reveal at least two populations with different origins. All fossil skulls after c.4500 B.C. found in Africa, Asia, and Europe resemble those of modern man. So do some Australian skulls from that period; but others, with backward-sloping foreheads, heavy brow ridges, and projecting jaws, recall earlier races.

❏ In the 20th century, Australian Aborigines united ancient crafts with modern materials. Some chipped out 'Stone Age' arrowheads from bottle glass, ceramic plates, and telegraph insulators. New interest in their traditional arts (above) may now promise a better future for the survivors of this much abused race.

❏ The Ainu – a people of unknown origin – inhabited Japan before the arrival of the 'modern' race. Physically unlike the Japanese, they are hirsute ('hairy Ainu'), with round, Caucasian-type eyes. Culturally, too, they are distinct: hunters and fishermen, they have never had a written language, and their religion centers on a bear cult. They were driven north over the centuries; today, a few survive in the northern island of Hokkaido, but their race is dying out.

Cities on the river

The Indus River Valley in South Asia was home in c.2500-1500 B.C. to the world's largest and most highly organized Bronze Age culture. The Indus civilization was based on agriculture and grew wealthy by trade, exporting its crop surplus. Perhaps it was the savage floods of the Indus that forced Stone Age farmers into a cooperative urban society, based upon astonishingly modern towns and cities. The standardization of town planning and the immense scale of such public buildings as granaries, where grain was gathered from across the kingdom, suggest an impressive central admininistration with high levels of communication. Each city comprises residential blocks intersected by broad main thoroughfares and narrower side streets. Houses are of uniform design, differing only in size, with such conveniences as private water supply, and bathrooms complete with brick-seated lavatories which empty into the main street drain. City drainage and sanitation systems bear comparison with present-day standards. Buildings damaged by flood or erosion were reconstructed in identical fashion as often as eight times over the centuries. Mysteriously, the culture came to an end c.1500 B.C., and the cities were gradually abandoned. Suggested reasons include alteration of the course of the Indus, attacks by nomadic invaders, or depletion of the valley's resources by over-intensive farming. For nearly 4,000 years the cities of the Indus Valley were lost from sight.

Merchants stamped their wares with seals carved from steatite, a hard stone, then baked and glazed. Each bears a brief pictographic text and emblem-design.

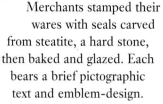

Cattle (above) were the major domestic animal; wild animals like elephants (left) are also a popular subject.

Behind the Great Bath lies a building with many rooms and corridors as well as several courtyards. This was perhaps a College, where scribes studied.

Mohenjo-Daro and Harappa yielded several small terracotta statuettes of a mysterious goddess, wearing loincloth, jewelry, and high headdress.

The Great Bath, one of Mohenjo-Daro's great civic buildings, was probably for ritual bathing, though other suggestions include a public swimming-pool – or a luxury brothel!

More than 1,200 of these fine seals have been found at Mohenjo-Daro alone, and a few as far away as southern Iraq.

Stone pillars mark the front of a range of rooms around the large communal bath. They may have been changing-rooms or priests' cells.

Few stone sculptures from the Indus civilization survive. This 7.5in (19 cm) limestone figure is one of 11 from Mohenjo-Daro. It depicts a priest-king or perhaps a god.

❑ The existence of the Indus civilization was unsuspected until 1921, when archaeologists exploring mounds at Harappa (Punjab) found a vast city. In 1922, c.340mi (550km) away, a site known as Mohenjo-Daro ('City of the Dead') was excavated to reveal a second city of strikingly similar design. It has been calculated that each was more than 3mi (4.8km) in circuit and housed c.30-40,000 people. More than 70 sites have since been explored by archaeologists.

❑ The lost religious beliefs of the Indus civilization may have left traces in the Hinduism of modern India. The many figurines and carvings of real and mythological animals suggest a reverence for animal life that reflects Hindu beliefs; a horned deity is shown seated in the yogic posture of the Hindu god Siva. If, as is thought, the Great Bath at Mohenjo-Daro was a place of public worship, this prefigures the Hindu practice of ritual washing before worship.

❑ In the Indus city of Mohenjo-Daro, a litter of broken clay vessels at a water-seller's stall suggests that clients threw their cups away after use – 4000 years before our disposable paper cups.

❑ The Indus people developed a pictographic script. Some 2,000 short inscriptions survive, mostly on carved seals, which were probably used in trade.

The pale invaders

The Indus civilization was already in decay in c.1500 B.C., when the Aryan tribes began their invasion of India. These nomadic horsemen, whose ancestors (the Indo-Europeans) came from the Russian steppe, made a series of inroads into India over a period of centuries. Although their culture was far less advanced than the urban and bureaucratic Indus civilization, it bequeathed to modern India a language (Sanskrit), many social customs (including the development of the caste system), and the foundation of the country's major religion, Hinduism. Aryan religious beliefs were recorded in hymns, which were passed on by word of mouth. The Bharata people preserved this tradition so faithfully that their hymns of 3,000 years ago are still in use today. Called the *Rig-Veda*, they are the most sacred of Hindu texts and are declaimed at weddings and funerals. By 900 B.C., Aryan priests were teaching that the world arose from the sacrificed body of a creator god (known to Hindus today as Brahma), and that only repeated acts of sacrifice would prevent a return to pre-creation chaos. They also developed the beginnings of belief in reincarnation and, later, the theory that people's lives are affected by good or bad actions in previous existences, doctrines fundamental to modern Hinduism. Hindus believe that each soul is reborn repeatedly until, by spiritual devotion, spiritual knowledge, or good works, it achieves liberation.

Hindu divinities intermingle with each other, reflecting the unity of all things. The figure's three heads reflect a multiple divinity.

Brahmani (early Hindu) sculpture of the 6th century A.D. Hinduism, still one of India's main religions, has roots in ancient Aryan beliefs.

5th-century A.D. Gupta carving of Vishnu, who, with Brahma and Shiva, makes up the Hindu trinity of supreme gods.

The emblem of sun deity Vishnu is the solar disk, Sudarsana, here portrayed personified as a youth.

Detail of sculpture at Hoysaleswara Temple (Mysore, India), dedicated to Shiva, Hindu god of destruction.

The layers of sculpture reflect movement upwards from the human to the divine. The lowest level is crowded with hundreds of animated figures; as the temple rises, the sculptures become less crowded and more serene.

The divine hero Krishna of Hindu legend is a prince and warrior, reflecting the caste structure of Aryan society. Hinduism remains a class-based religion.

Krishna is held to be the eighth, and most celebrated, incarnation of the god Vishnu, who took on human or animal forms to fight evil forces in the world.

FACT FILE

❑ Sacrifice was central to Aryan religion. They appeased the gods with offerings of drink (*soma*) poured on the ground. A rite that led to many wars was the horse sacrifice. A consecrated horse was allowed to wander freely for a year, followed by a band of warriors. Wherever it roamed, the local ruler had to pay homage to the Aryan king – or fight the warriors. At the end of the year, the horse was brought home and sacrificed.

❑ Aryan religion did not forbid people to enjoy the pleasures of life. Popular pastimes included drinking, dancing-girls, and song, as well as chariot-racing and gambling at dice. One of the few surviving non-religious poems of the time is a gambler's lament.

❑ The Aryans brought to India basic class-divisions between nobles, priests, and common men. Their scorn for the native people of India, whom they called *dasa* ('slaves'), fed class-consciousness to produce India's caste system. By c.500 B.C., society was divided into four broad classes which survive today: priests, warriors, peasants, and serfs.

❑ The famous sacred cows which roam India today owe their protected status to the fact that cattle formed the main livelihood – and measures of value – of the Aryan tribes. As such, they were venerated, and their meat was held taboo except for ritual meals.

Buddhism: doctrine of peace

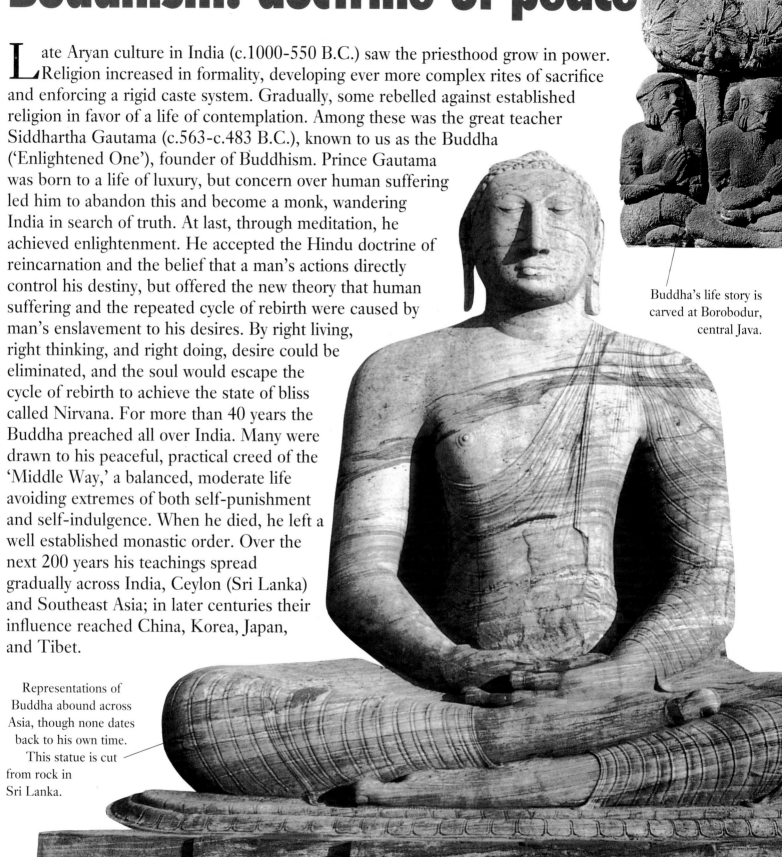

Late Aryan culture in India (c.1000-550 B.C.) saw the priesthood grow in power. Religion increased in formality, developing ever more complex rites of sacrifice and enforcing a rigid caste system. Gradually, some rebelled against established religion in favor of a life of contemplation. Among these was the great teacher Siddhartha Gautama (c.563-c.483 B.C.), known to us as the Buddha ('Enlightened One'), founder of Buddhism. Prince Gautama was born to a life of luxury, but concern over human suffering led him to abandon this and become a monk, wandering India in search of truth. At last, through meditation, he achieved enlightenment. He accepted the Hindu doctrine of reincarnation and the belief that a man's actions directly control his destiny, but offered the new theory that human suffering and the repeated cycle of rebirth were caused by man's enslavement to his desires. By right living, right thinking, and right doing, desire could be eliminated, and the soul would escape the cycle of rebirth to achieve the state of bliss called Nirvana. For more than 40 years the Buddha preached all over India. Many were drawn to his peaceful, practical creed of the 'Middle Way,' a balanced, moderate life avoiding extremes of both self-punishment and self-indulgence. When he died, he left a well established monastic order. Over the next 200 years his teachings spread gradually across India, Ceylon (Sri Lanka) and Southeast Asia; in later centuries their influence reached China, Korea, Japan, and Tibet.

Buddha's life story is carved at Borobodur, central Java.

Representations of Buddha abound across Asia, though none dates back to his own time. This statue is cut from rock in Sri Lanka.

The stupa (dome-shaped shrine) complex of Borobodur, built c.A.D. 800, is one of Buddhism's most spectacular monuments. This scene appears on one of its eight terraces, all of which are covered with elaborate carvings.

The young Prince Siddhartha, ahead of whom lies the quest for enlightenment which will transform him into the Buddha.

Ajanta, west India, boasts a group of 27 Buddhist cave sanctuaries, cut into the sides of a gorge. They belong to the Mauryan period (page 48) and feature murals and carvings of the Buddha.

The Buddha sits in the classic lotus posture of meditation developed in the East: back straight, legs crossed, hands resting loosely on knees.

The lotus flower on which Buddha sits is a common Buddhist image. In Japan, as symbol of Buddhist law, it came to be worshiped in its own right.

❑ Enlightenment came to the Buddha when he was seated under the Bodhi tree at Bodhgaya in southern Bihar. This became one of the holiest places of the Buddhist world. Cuttings from the tree were planted in other Buddhist lands, and a temple was raised at the site. The present temple at Bodhgaya is not the original, but dates from the Gupta period (c.A.D. 320-550).

❑ In Buddhist philosophy, life is symbolized by an ever-turning Wheel (below), which will revolve while ignorance lasts.

❑ In the 6th century B.C. many philosophers in India questioned the established religion, but only two alternative sects were to become independent religions. Buddhism was one; the other was Jainism, founded by the teacher Vardhamana (c.599-527 B.C.), called Mahavira ('Great Hero'). Like the Buddha, Mahavira rejected the rituals of Hinduism while retaining the concept of the cycle of rebirth. He called for a life of self-denial, and for non-violence to all creatures. Today, some 2 million Jains follow these teachings.

Ancient India's golden age

Alexander the Great's short-lived conquest of the Punjab region of northern India in 327 B.C. (see also *pages 70-71*) inspired a young warrior, Chandragupta Maurya, to build an empire of his own in India. Despite his low caste and comparatively small army, a series of carefully planned campaigns brought most of the north under his control in India's greatest ancient state: the Mauryan Empire of c.320-185 B.C. Farming and trade made the empire prosper. A network of well-made roads connected its towns, while a great trading road linked India with Persia through Afghanistan. By the time of Chandragupta's grandson, Ashoka, the Mauryan Empire had expanded to cover all India except the extreme south. Ashoka, emperor in c.274-c.236 B.C., was the greatest of the Mauryan rulers. For the first eight years he was a fierce war leader; but his violent conquest of the kingdom of Kalinga (Orissa), on the Bay of Bengal, sickened him with slaughter, and he resolved to rule peacefully and humanely. He made and enforced fair laws, seeking to unite his subjects through his policy of *Dhamma*, or universal social responsibility. The road of non-violence led him to Buddhism, and it was during his reign that Buddhist doctrines began to spread beyond India. All over India Ashoka's pillars of polished sandstone still stand, crowned with animal sculptures – often the lion symbol of Buddha – and inscribed with a record of his achievements and his creed of justice and mercy for all.

Elephants were captured and trained in the ancient Indian kingdoms before the Aryan invasions, and are a popular subject in art, and in both Hindu and Buddhist legend, through subsequent periods.

The Rock of Ashoka (Orissa, India) has been carved out to form an elephant.

The great stupa (Buddhist shrine) at Sanchi, northern India, was built in Ashoka's time, and became one of the principal Buddhist centers. Four great gateways were added over the next two centuries.

These panels, carved by the ivory-workers' guild, inspired the new Sanchi school of sculpture.

The gateposts are covered with detailed carvings. A panel from this post is enlarged (right).

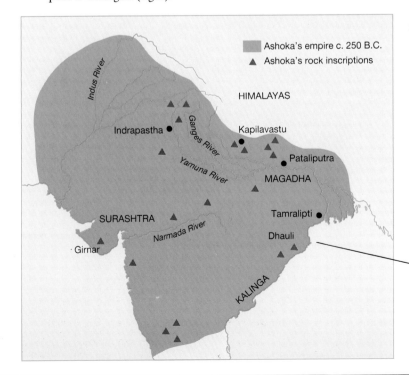

Ashoka's empire c. 250 B.C.
▲ Ashoka's rock inscriptions

Indus River
HIMALAYAS
Ganges River
Indrapastha ●
Kapilavastu
Yamuna River
Pataliputra ●
MAGADHA
SURASHTRA ▲
Tamralipti ●
Narmada River
Dhauli
Girnar
KALINGA

Sculpture in stone began in India with decorated stupa gateways, reflecting the Buddhist Order's growing wealth. It evolved from earlier work in wood and ivory.

Ashoka's empire extended over most of India, its boundaries still marked by inscribed rocks and pillars. He probably adopted the idea of recording his works on rocks from Greek-controlled Persia (modern Iran); the style of his pillars suggests that he imported craftsmen from that region.

FACT FILE

❏ When Ashoka became a Buddhist it was not only his human subjects who benefited. Instead of having several thousand animals killed daily for his kitchens, he reduced the 'meat menu' to a mere two peacocks and one gazelle each day. Later he became completely vegetarian.

❏ The complex Mauryan administrative system relied on espionage to keep the emperor informed of events and public opinion throughout his realm. Paid spies worked in the guise of holy hermits, householders, merchants, students, beggar women, and prostitutes.

❏ After Ashoka's death, the power of the Mauryan Empire declined. In c.185 BC, the last Mauryan emperor was overthrown – in one of history's first military coups – by one of his generals, Pushyamitra Sunga, who founded the Sunga dynasty. The powerful centralized monarchy became a federation of vassal kingdoms; some territories broke away to form independent states. Ashoka's policy of non-violence was forgotten, and wars broke out.

❏ Tradition has it that the founder of the Mauryan Empire, Chandragupta, converted to Jainism at the end of his reign. It is said he abdicated in favour of his son and traveled into south India as a Jain monk, ending his life by voluntary starvation – the Jain road to salvation.

African empires

'There is always something new out of Africa,' remarked the Roman writer Pliny (A.D. 23-79). Much of northern Africa was known territory to Greeks and Romans, but southward, many believed, lay lands inhabited by black giants (some said dwarfs) skilled in witchcraft. In fact, a civilization that would reach the height of its power as a Hamitic (black) empire began to evolve in what is now Sudan, along the southern Nile River, from c.3000 B.C. From c.2600 B.C. Egyptian forces raided and later occupied the gold-bearing territories of the land its dark skinned inhabitants called Kush.

But by c.1000 B.C. Kush was independent, and in c.730 B.C. the Kushite ruler Piankhi conquered Egypt. Kushite rule in Egypt (the 25th Dynasty) was short-lived: within 70 years an Assyrian invasion drove them south again. The Assyrians' iron weapons defeated the Kushites – but also gave them the knowledge of iron working. Centering on their capital at Napata, moved south to Meroë in c.530 B.C., the Kushites built a prosperous trading empire. Kush-Meroë (both names are used) was a predominantly black state, and may be called the first black African empire. Lying astride the main caravan routes, it exported agricultural and iron products. It was a way station for such exotic goods as ivory, animal skins, and ebony from equatorial Africa – and thus contributed to the spread of the skills of iron working among the black peoples farther south. Meroë escaped the domination of the Romans (who knew it as Nubia) in the 1st century A.D., only to fall in c.A.D. 350 to the Semitic people of Axum, (modern Ethiopia).

A Meroitic bust in sandstone, perhaps dating from the 2nd century A.D. These works were commemorative portraits, meant to be placed in small temples built above tombs.

Growing wealthy from their mines of gold and iron, the Kushites buried their rulers beneath Egyptian style pyramids in two cemeteries, of which this is one, at Meroe, their capital on the Nile.

Meroitic pyramids are small: most are between 50-100ft (15-30m) high. The buried kings do not lie inside the pyramids like Egyptian Pharaohs, but in large burial chambers excavated beneath them.

50

As the map shows, Kush, in the southern Nile valley, was ideally placed to benefit from trade. Caravans went up the Nile to Egypt; down the White Nile to equatorial Africa; west to the Sahara region; and east to Axum and the Red Sea.

Roman influence may be seen in the design of these pillars in the ruins of the 'Great Enclosure' at Musawwrat es-Sufra. It was built not long after Rome's invasion and brief occupation of Kush-Meroë in 23 B.C.

FACT FILE

❏ Iron smelting (slag heaps from ancient workings are still landmarks in the Sudan) and agriculture were the bases of Kush-Meroë's prosperity. Two ingenious devices – the *shaduf*, a pole with a bucket at one end, lifted by a counter weight; and the *saqia* (below), a large water wheel turned by oxen – enabled Kushite farmers to draw water from the Nile to irrigate their fields.

❏ Kush-Meroë's culture owed much to Egypt. At Meroë, some 60 small pyramids mark the tombs of its rulers. But the Kushites also developed their own arts and religious practices: their chief deity was Apedemek, who was portrayed with a lion's head, a human torso, and a serpent's body.

❏ Archaeologists have uncovered the remains of a huge complex of buildings, the 'Great Enclosure,' probably dating from the 1st century A.D., at Musawwarat es-Sufra, Sudan, near Meroë. Opinion is divided over whether it was a religious center, a royal palace, or a military training school (with a stable for war elephants). Inscriptions in the native Meroitic script still defy decipherment.

The Cretan civilization

The bull was a central image in art and religion. This head carved in black steatite (a hard stone) is a ritual vessel. Offerings of wine or water poured from the mouth when the head was lowered.

Europe's first major civilization was the Minoan culture, which flourished c.3000-1400 B.C. on the Mediterranean island of Crete. Its obscure beginnings lie in the early Bronze Age, when it was settled from Anatolia (Turkey), or possibly from Palestine. The islanders flourished as a sea people, by trade, fishing, and probably piracy, and before c.2000 B.C. had established a sophisticated and distinctive culture. From early pictographs they evolved a script known as Linear A, still undeciphered. Their craftsmen produced delicate metalwork, carved gemstones, and fine decorated pottery. Above all, the Minoans developed an elaborate architectural style, seen at its finest in vast palaces at Knossos, Mallia, and Phaestos.

Buildings several stories high were equipped with drainage systems as advanced as any before the A.D. 1700s; they had huge complexes of rooms, decorated with brilliant, animated frescoes, and linked by paved corridors and stone staircases. The Great Palace of Knossos spread over 6 acres (2.4ha) and may have housed c.40,000 people. The absence of fortifications suggests the Minoans had little fear of either internal warfare or invasion; from the latter, their naval power probably defended them. The greatest threat came from earthquakes: the mighty palaces were destroyed more than once, to be rebuilt more elaborately than before. But around 1400 B.C. the Minoan civilization came to an end, probably through a combination of widespread destruction caused by the volcanic eruption of the island of Thera in c.1450 B.C., and Mycenaean invasions from mainland Greece.

Fresco painting was the major art form of Minoan Crete. This fresco, reconstructed from the walls of the palace of Knossos, portrays acrobats leaping over a bull – probably a rite of the bull cult rather than a sport. Their wasp-waists and elaborate hairstyles are typical of Minoan palace fashion.

The sprawling ruins of Knossos reveal the wealth and splendor of the Minoan culture – and its reliance on industry and trade. Workshops and stores make up a large proportion of the palace complex.

An ideal, rather than an actual feat? Modern rodeo champions say bull-leaping as portrayed here is not humanly possible.

Huge earthenware jars in Knossos's storerooms could have held nearly 18,000gal (68,130l) of olive oil, a major Minoan export.

❑ The most mysterious Minoan relic is a round clay plate known as the Phaestos Disk (below). It is stamped on both sides with unique (and undeciphered) pictograms – the only example of 'printing' before the Chinese invented the process some 2,500 years later. No one has ever established the disk's function. Suggestions include a legal contract, a hymn, and an almanac.

❑ Greek mythology tells that King Minos of Crete kept a terrible bull-headed monster, the Minotaur, in a winding labyrinth below his palace at Knossos. In 1900, British archaeologist Sir Arthur Evans discovered the remains of a vast Bronze Age palace at Knossos – and the probable basis of the legend. The palace itself, with its maze of corridors and rooms, may well have been the original labyrinth; evidence of a religious cult centering on the bull suggests the origins of the mythical Minotaur.

Mycenae: city of the lion

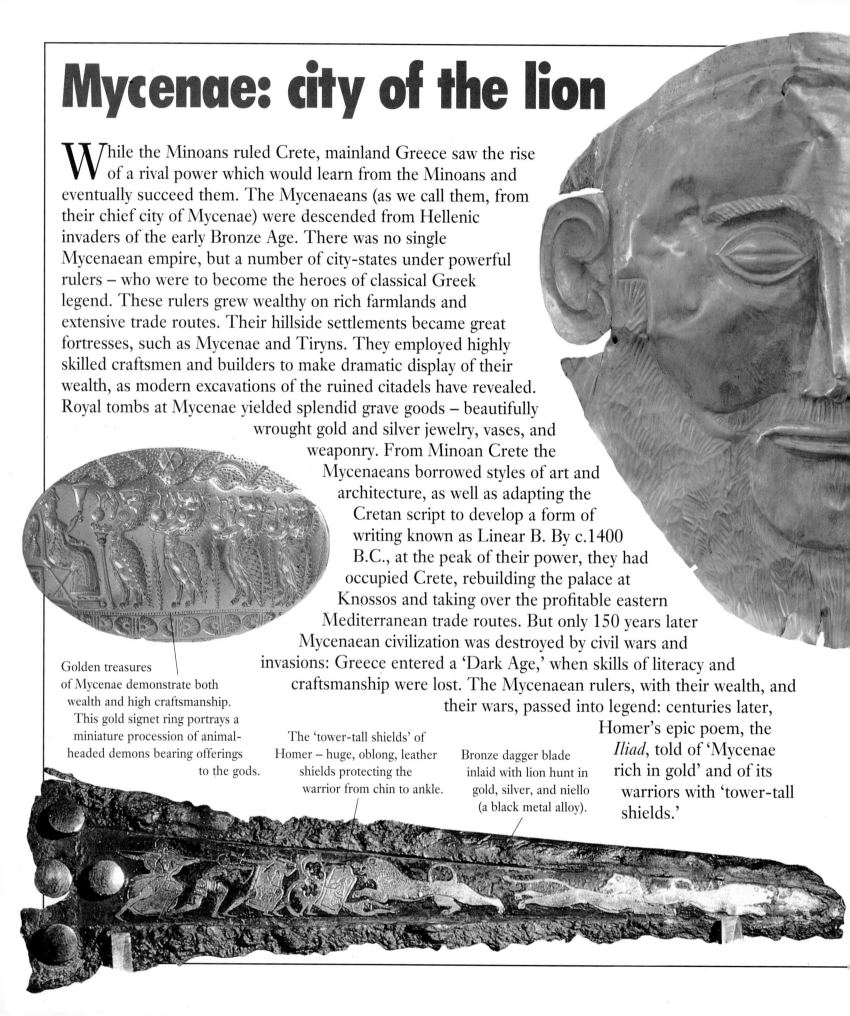

While the Minoans ruled Crete, mainland Greece saw the rise of a rival power which would learn from the Minoans and eventually succeed them. The Mycenaeans (as we call them, from their chief city of Mycenae) were descended from Hellenic invaders of the early Bronze Age. There was no single Mycenaean empire, but a number of city-states under powerful rulers – who were to become the heroes of classical Greek legend. These rulers grew wealthy on rich farmlands and extensive trade routes. Their hillside settlements became great fortresses, such as Mycenae and Tiryns. They employed highly skilled craftsmen and builders to make dramatic display of their wealth, as modern excavations of the ruined citadels have revealed. Royal tombs at Mycenae yielded splendid grave goods – beautifully wrought gold and silver jewelry, vases, and weaponry. From Minoan Crete the Mycenaeans borrowed styles of art and architecture, as well as adapting the Cretan script to develop a form of writing known as Linear B. By c.1400 B.C., at the peak of their power, they had occupied Crete, rebuilding the palace at Knossos and taking over the profitable eastern Mediterranean trade routes. But only 150 years later Mycenaean civilization was destroyed by civil wars and invasions: Greece entered a 'Dark Age,' when skills of literacy and craftsmanship were lost. The Mycenaean rulers, with their wealth, and their wars, passed into legend: centuries later, Homer's epic poem, the *Iliad*, told of 'Mycenae rich in gold' and of its warriors with 'tower-tall shields.'

Golden treasures of Mycenae demonstrate both wealth and high craftsmanship. This gold signet ring portrays a miniature procession of animal-headed demons bearing offerings to the gods.

The 'tower-tall shields' of Homer – huge, oblong, leather shields protecting the warrior from chin to ankle.

Bronze dagger blade inlaid with lion hunt in gold, silver, and niello (a black metal alloy).

❏ The Mycenaeans left many clay tablets inscribed in Linear B. When this was finally deciphered in 1952, the tablets proved to be storeroom records. More importantly, they proved that the Mycenaeans were Greek-speaking and therefore the true ancestors of the classical Greeks.

❏ The Greeks of classical times believed that the ruined fortresses of the Mycenaeans were the work of giants. This type of masonry, using huge irregular stones, is still called cyclopean – after the mythical giant Cyclops.

❏ In the 1870s the poetry of Homer, telling of King Agamemnon of Mycenae, inspired archaeologist Heinrich Schliemann to excavate the ruins of Mycenae and Troy. He identified his splendid finds with individuals from Homeric legend – with more enthusiasm than accuracy. A superb gold death mask led him to claim, 'I have gazed on the face of Agamemnon.' The 'Mask of Agamemnon' actually predates that ruler by some 300 years.

❏ The vast 'beehive tombs' of Mycenaean rulers were beehive-shaped stone chambers up to 50ft (15m) high. These palaces for the dead required great masonic skill as well as hard labor: such large chambers, without pillars to support the domed roofs, were unrivaled in Europe for some 1500 years.

The so-called 'Mask of Agamemnon,' a death mask of beaten gold from Mycenae, actually dates from c.1550 B.C., three centuries before Agamemnon's time. Shaft graves at Mycenae held a wealth of gold, silver, bronze, crystal, and alabaster.

The Lion Gate, Mycenae. Mycenaean citadels were fortified with massive walls, on average 15ft (4.5m) thick, and faced with huge irregular stones, replaced by square blocks for strength at gateways – an attacker's main target.

The Mycenaean world – a collection of allied kingdoms rather than a unified state – began as a mainland culture, and was influenced from early days by that of Minoan Crete. With the takeover of the Minoan sea trade, its sphere of influence expanded to include most of the Aegean islands.

Troy

AEGEAN SEA

Delphi

Athens

Mycenae

RHODES

MEDITERRANEAN SEA

CRETE

55

The Trojan War

The campaign in which the Mycenaean Greeks destroyed the great city of Troy (known to them as Ilion, or Ilium), is one of the best known wars in history. For centuries Homer's *Iliad*, an epic poem telling of the war's final year, has been a worldwide best seller, inspiring hundreds of later writers (from Shakespeare to movie screen-writers) to retell its story. Yet we cannot be certain that the war was ever fought, or that Homer ever wrote. Archaeological work pioneered by Heinrich Schliemann (1822-90) shows that between c.3000 B.C. and the early Christian era some 10 settlements stood on Hissarlik mound in modern Turkey. Homeric Troy was probably the seventh, a fortress dominating the Hellespont, a vital trade channel between the Black Sea and Mediterranean. Homer says the kidnaping of Helen, wife of Menelaus of Sparta, by the Trojan Paris, brought a Greek expeditionary force headed by Agamemnon of Mycenae to besiege Troy. If Homer's armada did sail, it was probably to break Troy's grip on the Hellespont. Homer's battle scenes are magnificent: Achilles, Hector, and other champions thunder on to the field in two-horse chariots and dismount to engage in single combat, first hurling their spears, then closing with swords. In the war's tenth year, cunning Odysseus's ruse of the Wooden Horse leads to the fall of Troy's 'topless towers.' It is possible that Troy VII was sacked around 1260 B.C.; equally, it may have been destroyed by an earthquake. Both horses and earthquakes are associated with the sea-god Poseidon, so Homer's account may be an example of 'poetic licence.'

This fearsome fighter may be the Greek champion Achilles. Homer tells how, mad with rage at the death of his comrade Patroclus, he slew Hector and then mutilated his body (a foul crime in ancient religious belief).

Threatened by his enemy's spear, a warrior, perhaps Hector of Troy, attempts to guard himself with his shield: a vase painting of the 4th-5th century B.C.

According to legend (but not to Homer), 'superhero' Achilles had only one weak spot, his heel. He died when Paris of Troy found this mark with a poisoned arrow.

Although Homer says the kidnaping of beautiful Helen provoked the war, it was probably fought (if at all) over trading routes.

Paris entertains Helen with music: an 18th century artist's fanciful view of the lovers who 'launched a thousand ships.'

Bronze or leather helmets, maybe crested as seen here, protected those who fought at Troy.

Noble featured and with sightless eyes, this bust is a traditional portrayal of Homer, bard of the Trojan War. The poems were not written down until centuries had passed.

The Trojan War story was retold thousands of times. Some 2,000 years after Homer, British chroniclers wrote a sequel, with Trojan refugee Brutus and his men ending up in Britain – hence its name.

FACT FILE

❏ According to tradition, the blind bard Homer begged his way through seven Greek cities (all anxious to claim him as a native when he was dead and famous) in the 9th century B.C. For centuries scholars have argued whether Homer was one man (or woman), two, more, or whether he existed at all.

❏ The *Iliad* inspired the Latin poet Vergil to write the *Aeneid* (30-19 B.C.). It tells how Aeneas of Troy escaped from the burning city and, after many wanderings, reached Italy and founded Lavinium, forerunner of Rome itself.

❏ Trojan War champions regarded the spear as the major weapon: Hector, says Homer, wielded one 18ft (5.5m) long. Their bronze swords were not durable in long combat; their bows probably had an effective range of only c.50yd (15m). For protection they had shields made of layers of bull's hide, and helmets, breastplates, and greaves (leggings), of bronze or leather (below). They knew of iron, but generally used it only for arrow tips or non-military items.

Gods of Olympus

Mount Olympus, Greece's highest peak, was revered in classical times as the home of the gods. The Olympian deities were the product of thousands of years and a number of cultures. The forerunners of the Greeks, like most early farming societies, had worshiped a Mother Goddess, patron of fertility and the harvest. After 2000 B.C., Hellenic invaders introduced the Indo-European sky-god Zeus, who was to become the supreme god of classical Greece. The Mother cult was absorbed into what became the pantheon of Greek gods. Under the name of Hera ('the Lady'), the Mother goddess became the consort of Zeus; her other aspects contributed to Aphrodite, goddess of love; Artemis, virgin huntress, a goddess of wild nature; Athene, goddess of war and also of wisdom and crafts; and Demeter, the corn goddess. The gods of Olympus included Poseidon, god of the sea; Hephaestus, the smith god; Apollo, patron of the arts and medicine; Ares, god of war; and Hermes, messenger between gods and men. Beyond Olympus, the Underworld (realm of the dead) was ruled by Hades with his consort Persephone. Zeus, dispenser of justice, ruled over all. The gods were worshiped at hundreds of small local shrines as well as vast marble temples like the Parthenon in Athens. The many religious festivals were times of rejoicing as well as solemn worship. The Olympic Games were part of the great festival of Zeus. At the orgiastic celebrations of Dionysos, god of wine (a late addition to the Greek pantheon), his female followers, the Maenads ('wild women') were said to roam the mountains tearing wild beasts and even men to pieces.

Zeus stands poised to hurl his thunderbolt – the divine weapon made for him by the Cyclopes, storm-spirits – at any who oppose his will. Thunder and lightning represented the wrath of the gods to many ancient cultures.

Zeus, king of the gods, ruled the universe. His powers were limited by the laws of fate, but he designed the good or bad destiny of all individuals.

A satyr – a woodland demon, half god, half beast. Satyrs, notoriously lustful and drunken, are the regular associates of wine god Dionysos.

Dionysos leans drunkenly on the satyr. The orgiastic rites of the Greek wine god shocked Rome, which banned his cult in 186 B.C., executing thousands of his worshipers.

The destructive aspect of this god of fruitfulness and frenzy is symbolized by one of his animal emblems, the leopard.

A sacrifice is laid on the altar, honoring the herm, a stone pillar sacred to Hermes the messenger-god. He was patron of travelers; passers-by invoked his pillars for good fortune.

The herm, shaped like an erect penis surmounted by the god's head, stood outside the Greek home.

The Temple of Apollo, Corinth. The Classical Greek temple, with its characteristic rectangular shape and massive pillars, was built as a house for the god, not a place for worship. Only priests entered: worshipers gathered at an altar outside.

FACT FILE

❑ The poet Homer portrays the Olympians as a quarrelsome and all too human family, prey to the same faults and weaknesses as men. Among themselves they constantly indulge in intrigues and adulteries; in their dealings with humans they are often less than just, picking out favorites or enemies among mortals.

❑ The Greeks sought guidance from the gods by way of some 250 oracles. Most famous was that of Delphi (above), where the Pythia (priestess) relayed the gods' answers – which were often ambiguous. Croesus of Lydia was told: 'If Croesus crosses the Halys River, he will destroy a mighty empire.' He did, and was defeated: the empire he destroyed was his own.

❑ One god often had several aspects. At Delphi, Apollo was worshiped as Phoebus Apollo, the sun god, whose rays both caused and cured the plague. In Arcadia, as Apollo Lykanthropos the wolf god, he received sacrifices of human flesh.

The wonders of the world

We remember certain achievements of the Ancient World as the 'Seven Wonders of the World.' The most mysterious was the Colossus of Rhodes (c.300 B.C.), a giant bronze figure said to have stood astride the harbor entrance (more probably at the harbor side). The sculptor Phidias (c.490-417 B.C.) made the marble statue of Jupiter (Zeus) for the temple at Olympia. The Temple of Diana (Artemis) at Ephesus, built c.600-501 B.C., was burned down in c.356 B.C. by one Herostratus, who hoped to make his name remembered (and unfortunately succeeded!) by this act of vandalism. In c.280 B.C., Sostratus of Cnidus built a lighthouse more than 300ft (91m) high on the island of Pharos, to guide ships into the harbor of Alexandria. It endured until A.D. 1346, when earthquake damage forced its demolition. The famous Hanging Gardens of Babylon were created in c.605 B.C. for King Nebuchadrezzar at the heart of his rebuilt city. The monumental tomb of Mausoleus of Caria, built by his widow in 363-361 B.C., became known as the Mausoleum of Halicarnassus. Fragments of its superb sculptures are all that remain. The oldest and longest lasting is the tomb of the Egyptian Pharoah Cheops (Khufu), the Great Pyramid at Gizeh (c.2600 B.C.), for more than 4,000 years the world's tallest building and designed with such mathematical and engineering skills that its four planes face precisely north, south, east, and west. It is the only one of the Seven Wonders now surviving.

Tradition, and most reconstructions, of the Colossus of Rhodes set it astride the harbor, but most authorities now consider this unlikely.

It took vast material and labor resources, and most of Cheops' 23 year reign, to build his Great Pyramid. It comprises some 2,300,000 stone blocks, averaging 2.5 tons each and some up to 15 tons in weight.

Assyrian relief from 693 B.C., portraying King Ashurbanipal and his queen feasting in the splendor of Nebuchadrezzar's Hanging Gardens.

The luxurious 'garden rooms' of the Hanging Gardens looked out on sloping terraces filled with exotic plants and huge trees. The gardens were maintained by a complex mechanical irrigation system to draw up water from the Euphrates River.

As well as his own pyramid, Cheops built three smaller pyramids to inter his wives in slightly lesser splendor beside him.

❏ The Colossus of Rhodes represented the sun god Helios. It is said to have been more than 100ft (30m) tall, and that ships could sail between its legs. It was built to commemorate the merchant city's successful resistance to a year-long siege; some 50 years later it was destroyed by an earthquake.

❏ The statue of Jupiter by Phidias was about 40ft (12.2m) high and was inlaid with gold, ivory, and jewels. Phidias is believed to have worked on the famous sculptures of the Parthenon in Athens. His Jupiter was destroyed in the 5th century A.D.

❏ In the 1st century B.C., Hero of Alexandria designed a fire-engine, with water tank and two-cylinder force-pump.

❏ The Hanging Gardens of Babylon were built as an integral part of the royal apartments and were only accessible through these. They were built on stone arches c.75ft (23m) above the ground and strong enough to bear great weights of soil. The galleries beneath the arches formed luxurious 'garden rooms' for Nebuchadrezzar.

❏ 2000 years after the Great Pyramid was built, Greek historian Herodotus recorded inscriptions on its side 'telling how much was spent on radishes, onions, and garlic for the workmen' – probably actually a list of food offerings.

The golden age of Athens

Greek civilization faltered during the Dark Age that followed the splendor of the Mycenaean era. But from c.800 B.C. a period of new development (the Archaic Period) saw the emergence of an influential Greek culture, based on a number of small, independent city-states. Greatest of these was Athens, which during the Classical Age (c.500-323 B.C.) was a center of intellectual and cultural development that has been called 'the nursery of western civilization.' Playwrights, historians, and scientists gathered here. Philosophers challenged established ideas about the nature of the universe: they sought rational explanations to replace myths, and made great advances in sciences, math, and medicine.

Only the shell of the Parthenon, Athena's great temple, remains, but its balance and proportions make it world renowned. Built in 447-4387 B.C., it housed a gold and ivory image of the goddess, destroyed in ancient times.

People flocked to Athens to hear the words of its greatest philosophers: Socrates (469-399 B.C.); his pupil Plato (427-347 B.C.); and Plato's follower Aristotle (384-322 B.C.). Athens led the Greek states in creating laws fair to rich and poor alike, and, under rulers like Solon (c.640-c.559 B.C.) and Pesistratos (c.600-527 B.C.), moved towards replacing the rule of a few rich individuals with the first 'democracy.' All adult male citizens of Athens had the right to vote on matters concerning the making of laws and the election of rulers. The Athenian government employed Greece's finest architects and sculptors to provide the city with splendid public buildings – temples, monuments, and theaters. The Parthenon, whose ruins still crown Athens, is considered the perfect example of the Classical style of architecture, which exerts both esthetic and technical influence to this day.

Athenian statesman Pericles (c.490-429 B.C.) pursued military ends in preparing for war with Sparta, and a more enduring goal: to make Athens the cultural center of the world. His great building program included the Parthenon temple.

An architectural trick: a tiny convex curve makes the columns look straighter than straight.

Philosopher Socrates (469-399 B.C.) held himself 'midwife of men's thoughts' – but was condemned to death for impiety.

In 1816 the British government bought the Elgin Marbles, a group of superb carvings from the Parthenon and the largest group of classical Greek sculpture surviving. Their possible return to Greece has been the subject of heated debate.

❑ Classical Greek architecture began with rectangular stone temples supported by massive columns. The earliest and most persistent style, Doric, has stubby, fluted columns with plain capitals; the later, more elaborate, Ionic has slimmer columns with curled capitals.

❑ Athenian democracy was for free, male Athenians only. Neither slaves nor foreigners could benefit – and Athenian women led a 'life in the shadows,' rarely allowed out of their homes and denied both political rights and education.

❑ Education (for men) was highly valued. From the age of seven, boys of wealthy families attended schools which taught reading, writing, music, athletics, and preparation for civic life. At 14 they could progress to *gymnasia* to study science, math, and public speaking. At 18 they began two years' military training.

❑ The term 'academy' for a place of learning comes from the Academos school (named after a hero of myth) at Athens where Plato taught (below).

The glory that was Greece

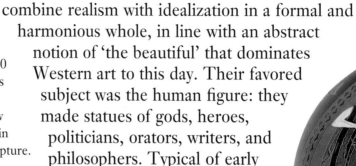

'Beauty in visible things, as in everything else, consists of symmetry and proportion.' Thus the philosopher Plotinus (A.D. 205-270) summarized the guiding rules of classical Greek art. Artists aimed to combine realism with idealization in a formal and harmonious whole, in line with an abstract notion of 'the beautiful' that dominates Western art to this day. Their favored subject was the human figure: they made statues of gods, heroes, politicians, orators, writers, and philosophers. Typical of early Greek statuary are *kouroi*, figures of naked youths. Early *kouroi* are very formal. They hold identical stiff poses, staring straight ahead, and wear the same expression, lips curved in the 'archaic smile.' By the Classical period, increasing anatomical knowledge led to techniques that enabled sculptors to create more lifelike figures in natural poses. The 'archaic smile' was replaced by an expression of detached calm. Sculptors pursued an ideal of beauty. The male ideal was portrayed naked because male nudity was common. Women (other than goddesses) were shown clothed because modesty of dress was part of the female ideal. This enabled sculptors to develop to the full the skill of carving draperies. The human figure was also portrayed in painting, and painted vases are among the great works of Greek artists. As in sculpture, early paintings are stiffly representational; later, theories of balance and symmetry were brought to bear. The figures, isolated against an empty background, often depict scenes from the heroic tales of the *Iliad* and *Odyssey* in a fluid and dramatic style.

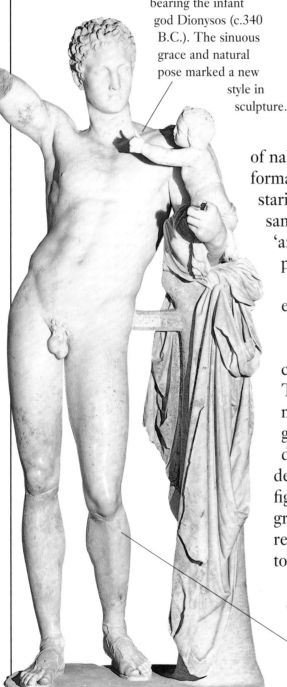

The classical ideal of male beauty: statue of the god Hermes bearing the infant god Dionysos (c.340 B.C.). The sinuous grace and natural pose marked a new style in sculpture.

Only surviving work of Praxiteles, Athenian master sculptor, famed for his emphasis on human beauty when portraying the gods. Indeed, his Aphrodite (known from a Roman copy) was modeled on his mistress, Phryne.

Wine vase, with painted black-figure decoration. Painted pottery was a favourite Greek art form. Pots were painted before a three-stage firing process which fixed the colors.

The famous Nike, or Winged Victory, of Samothrace, shows carved draperies at their finest: contrasted swirls and clinging folds express movement. The figure of Victory, alighting on a ship's prow, commemorates a naval triumph.

The pot was thinly coated with specially treated clay, on which the design was painted with denser black clay. Any detail was then incised, or painted with purple or white paint (as here), before the pot was fired.

The filigree flowers and spirals of this gold pendant are typical of classical Greek jewelry, as is the use of granulation (a design in minute gold spheres, often under 0.02in (5mm) diameter).

❏ From 600 B.C. Athenian vase painters were supreme in black-figure painting. They painted black designs on a red clay ground, incising line details before the clay was fired. By 530 B.C., they had invented red-figure painting, leaving the design in the natural color of the clay, and painting the ground black. Detail was drawn in black paint, finer than before. This technique replaced black-figure painting.

❏ Greek jewelers, too, were master craftsmen. Goldsmiths created fine filigree work in spirals, waves, and floral sprays. As well as delicate necklaces, bracelets, and earrings, they crafted gold or silver versions of the wreaths worn by victors at the games. The Greeks loved color – their statues were often painted – and jewelers often embellished their work with bright enamels and gemstones: blood-red garnets were especially popular.

❏ The 'Venus de Milo' (or Aphrodite of Melos), now in the Louvre, Paris, was sculpted by Alexandros of Antioch in c.150 B.C. It is acknowledged to be one of the greatest masterpieces of ancient art, an ideal of feminine beauty. Irreverent modern writers have pointed out that the Venus's body measurements would make her a dress size 16-18 – 'outsize' by the standards imposed by today's fashion setters.

The players and the games

Two of our great legacies from Greece, theater and organized sport, were rooted in religious festivals. Thespis, an Athenian poet of the 6th century B.C., is said to have originated drama by introducing into choral rites a 'commentator' on the words of the choir. (Actors are still sometimes called 'Thespians.') True drama was developed by Aeschylus (c.525-456 B.C.) and Sophocles (c.496-406 B.C.), who added more characters, the 'realistic' tragedian Euripides (c.480-405 B.C.), and Aristophanes (c.450-388 B.C.), father of comedy. The Olympic Games were held every four years at Olympia, shrine of Zeus. Traditionally begun in 776 B.C., they imposed a 'sacred truce' on rival tribes, whose champions competed in a stadium holding c.20,000 spectators. Early Olympics centered on foot races: the *stade* (one length of the stadium; c.220yd/200m), *diaulos* (c.440yd/400m), and *dolichos* (c.3mi/5,000m). Soon were added the *pentathlon* (a five-event competition: *stade*, long jump, discus and javelin throwing, wrestling); the *pancration* (boxing and wrestling); and horse and chariot racing. Although the official prize was a crown of olive leaves, winners were richly rewarded by their own people: Athenian victors in the 5th century B.C. got cash equivalent to about $50,000 and were excused taxes. After the Roman conquest of the 2nd century B.C., professionalism, use of drugs to improve performance, and spectator hooliganism increased. In A.D. 393, Emperor Theodosius I, a Christian who disapproved the 'pagan' emphasis on bodily rather than spiritual health, banned the Olympics.

An illustration based on an ancient sculpture shows a competitor in the *pancration* – the boxing-wrestling competition introduced in c.688 B.C. – whose hands are protected by leather bands.

Strolling players – like this performer on the crotales, metal finger cymbals – provided popular entertainment from the earliest times.

Masked entertainers shown in a mosaic of around the 1st century B.C. remind us that the theater originated in music and dance. The woman blows a double flute, a type of instrument that dates back at least to the early Iron Age.

A charioteer takes the reins. Races for four-horse chariots (quadrigas) featured in the Olympics from 680 B.C.; chariots drawn by two horses did not appear in the Games until 408 B.C.

A street musician capers to the beat of his tambourine, one of the oldest of musical instruments and virtually unchanged today.

Greek horse breeds were generally too small, averaging only c.14 hands (4.7ft/1.4m) in height, to make good riding mounts.

Victors in the earliest Games were given crowns of olive leaves. By the 3rd century A.D., the date of this gold Olympic medal, rewards were richer.

❏ The main 'field events' at the Greek Olympics were discus and javelin. The stone discus weighed up to 13lb (5.9kg) and its thrower probably stood still, so the event was more a test of strength than of skill and agility, as with the modern 'turning' throw. The wooden javelin was thrown 'on the run,' as today.

❏ Records showing a distance of c.55ft (16.8m) covered in the ancient Olympic long jump suggest that it consisted of a series of standing jumps. The 'standing long jump' (record distance: 11.4ft/3.47m) featured in the modern Olympics until 1912.

❏ No woman could compete in the Olympics, and married women were barred from the *altis*, the sacred enclosure in which Zeus's temple and the stadium stood. Women had their own four-yearly Heraean Games (honoring Hera, queen of the gods), where, like the men at Olympia, they competed naked.

❏ By the 1st century B.C., sport had become 'professionalized' to the extent that Greek athletes formed trades unions (*xistus*) to negotiate prize money with the promoters of games.

❏ Greek sprinters used simple 'starting blocks.' A runner making a false start risked a whipping, and later a mechanical starting gate (*husplex*) appeared.

Sparta: a military elite

'Go, tell the Spartans, you who pass us by, That here obedient to their laws we lie.' This was the epitaph, attributed to Simonides (556-468 B.C.), on the grave mound of King Leonidas of Sparta and his soldiers at Thermopylae. Here, in 480 B.C., c.7,000 Greeks attempted to hold a narrow pass against 100,000 Persian invaders under King Xerxes. In a rearguard stand, Leonidas and 300 Spartans fought to the death, true to the military law of their nation. With an economy based on a large, sternly controlled, slave class ('helots'), Spartiates (free citizens) devoted themselves to military training from the age of seven. Coming-of-age rites included savage floggings: a boy who showed he felt pain was branded a weakling and coward. Traditionally long haired, wearing red cloaks, and marching to flute music, Spartan *hoplites* – heavy infantry, well armored and carrying long spears, maneuvering in the mass formation called the phalanx – became the military elite of Greece.

But although they led the successful resistance to the Persian invasions, they were disliked and feared by many Greeks. In the Peloponnesian War (431-404 B.C.), Sparta clashed with Athens. Athens was victorious at sea, but suffered heavy defeats on land, notably in the siege of Syracuse (416 B.C.), where a Spartan general, Gylippus, rallied local troops. Sparta was finally victorious, but the state's extreme conservatism – its distrust of new ideas and its refusal to expand the Spartiate class by admitting new citizens – led to its decline from the 4th century B.C.

Bronze armor like that worn by hoplites around the 5th century B.C.: cuirass (body armor), greaves (leggings), and helmet.

Syracusan coin shows Victory crowning a charioteer.
At Syracuse in 416 B.C., Athens was defeated by Sicilian naval and land forces under a Spartan general, Gylippus.

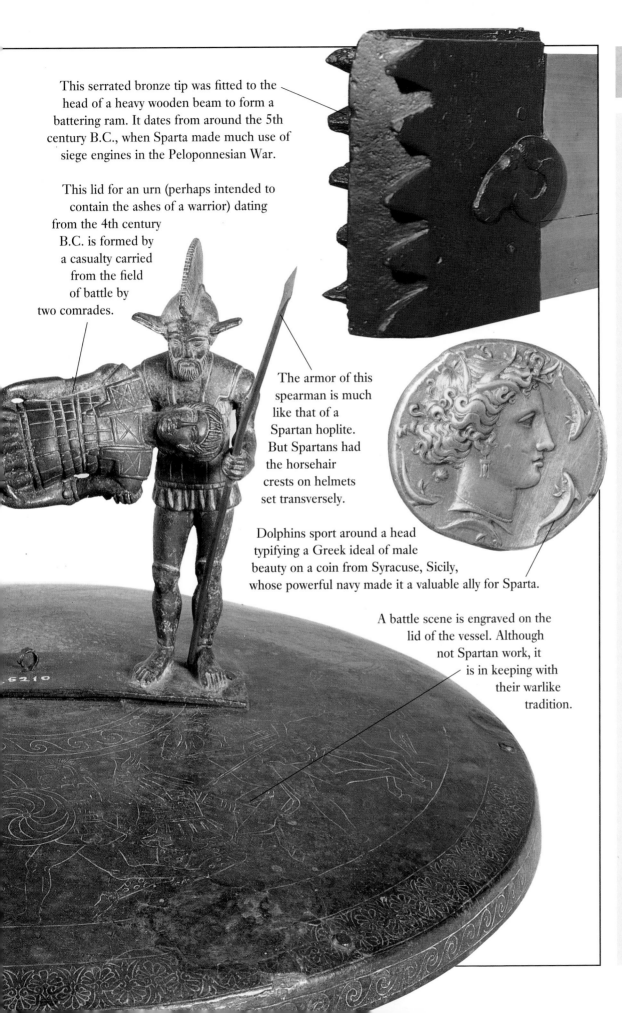

This serrated bronze tip was fitted to the head of a heavy wooden beam to form a battering ram. It dates from around the 5th century B.C., when Sparta made much use of siege engines in the Peloponnesian War.

This lid for an urn (perhaps intended to contain the ashes of a warrior) dating from the 4th century B.C. is formed by a casualty carried from the field of battle by two comrades.

The armor of this spearman is much like that of a Spartan hoplite. But Spartans had the horsehair crests on helmets set transversely.

Dolphins sport around a head typifying a Greek ideal of male beauty on a coin from Syracuse, Sicily, whose powerful navy made it a valuable ally for Sparta.

A battle scene is engraved on the lid of the vessel. Although not Spartan work, it is in keeping with their warlike tradition.

FACT FILE

❑ Spartiates always feared a slave revolt. In 425 B.C., 2,000 helots who had apparently saved a Spartan force from destruction were promised their freedom, then massacred. The Spartiates had faked the emergency to discover which helots were bravest – and therefore should be killed before they planned revolt.

❑ Spartan hoplites' greatest victory was at Plateae in 479 B.C., where their charge smashed the Persian 'Immortals' – an elite force, so called because when one fell another equally efficient replaced him – and ended Persia's threat to Greece.

❑ Athens' sea victories in the Peloponnesian War were won by galleys. The Athenian trireme was c.130ft (40m) long, but only c.15ft (4.6m) in beam. Some 170 rowers (freemen, not slaves) pulled 15ft (4.6m) long oars. The rowers kept their strokes in time not to the beat of a drum (as shown in most historical movies) but to the sound of a flute player. They were armed with missile weapons: javelins and slings. Only about 20 hoplites and archers were carried: the favored tactic was ramming rather than boarding.

❑ We remember Sparta in the phrase 'a Spartan lifestyle' (simple and highly disciplined) and the word 'laconic' (close mouthed; Spartans, also called Laconians, traditionally preferred actions to words).

Alexander: master of the world

Military power in Greece passed in the 4th century B.C. to the northern kingdom of Macedonia. The phalangists (heavy infantry) of King Philip II (382-336), armed with the *sarissa*, a 15ft (4.6m) spear, their flanks protected by light infantry (*hypaspists*) and cavalry, brought most of Greece under his control. With his murder – possibly arranged by his wife Olympias – in 337, his army, and his plans for eastward expansion, passed to his son, Alexander III 'The Great' (356-323 B.C.). In 333 Alexander marched against the great empire of Darius III of Persia, crushing its armies at Issus. He swept south through Phoenicia to conquer Egypt and to found the city of Alexandria. Turning east, he urged on his soldiers (fewer than half native Macedonians; mercenaries flocked to his standard) to complete the conquest of Asia Minor and at last strike into India. With the annihilation of Indian King Porus's army on the Hydaspes (modern Jhelum) River in 326, yet another subcontinent lay open to him. But his men, having marched c.21,000 miles (33,800km) in 10 years' campaigning, would go no farther. In 323, burned out by his superhuman feats, Alexander died at Babylon. His empire (large as the modern U.S.A.) was divided between his chief generals, among them Ptolemy (c.367-283 B.C.), who took Egypt and founded the dynasty that ended with Cleopatra in 30 B.C. Alexander's greatness lay not only in his conquests, which quadrupled the size of the Greek world, but the manner of them. He did not destroy the societies he subjugated, but married their best aspects with those of Hellenic civilization, thus leaving a lasting mark on world culture.

Bust of Alexander (always portrayed clean shaven, although he was certainly bearded): an ancient copy of a work attributed to Lysippus, greatest Greek sculptor of Alexander's age.

His coinage presents an idealized head of Philip II, father of Alexander. A war wound had left him lacking one eye, his face badly scarred.

Empire of Alexander the Great

The map shows the enormous extent of Alexander's short lived empire. Had he lived, it is said, he planned to 'Hellenicize' the world by resettling Greek peoples in Asia and Asian peoples in the West.

A Roman mosaic based on an ancient Greek painting shows King Darius III of Persia in the moment of defeat at Issus.

A spearman of Alexander's elite 'Companion' cavalry attacks an Indian warrior mounted on an elephant. This Macedonian coin was probably struck to mark the victory on the Hydaspes River, 326 B.C.

Darius may have had c.100,000 men at Issus, to Alexander's c.35,000. Darius's hired Greek hoplites fought well, but Alexander's heavy cavalry turned the battle.

❑ Many legends attest Alexander's courage and determination. As a child, it was said, he was the only Macedonian able to tame the great stallion Bucephalus ('Bull Head'), which became his warhorse – and one of the ancient world's costlier mounts: King Philip is said to have paid 16 talents of gold (now around $25,000) for him. Bucephalus died aged 30, of wounds received in the battle of the Hydaspes. Told of a prophecy that whoever unraveled the complex 'Gordian Knot' would rule all Asia, Alexander drew his sword and cut it apart with one stroke.

❑ By the 4th century B.C., armies such as Alexander's were equipped with 'artillery.' This took the form of portable missile launchers such as the *oxybeles* ('dart shooter'), sending a heavy arrow to c.500yd (450m), and the *lithobolos* ('stone thrower'), hurling a boulder of up to 180lb (82kg) and effective against fortifications from c.200yd (185m). These were torsion weapons, powered by stretched and twisted ropes.

❑ Alexander died at the age of 32. We may see that as an early death – but it was around the average life span in the classical world. The average life expectancy of a Roman male born c.A.D. 1 has been estimated at 36 years: by A.D. 1400, in the Italy of the early Renaissance, the figure had risen only to c.38 years.

71

The Celtic tribes of Europe

Iron Age central and western Europe saw the advance of the Celts. From c.600 B.C., the Hallstatt culture (so called from a major archaeological site) brought these pastoral nomads to prominence. A warrior people, well equipped with domesticated horses (then rare in Europe) and efficient iron weapons, they quickly gained control of trade routes between Europe and the Mediterranean coast, and set up great hilltop fortresses at strategic points. From c.450 B.C., the second Celtic phase, called the La Tène culture, saw their major migrations. Some tribes raided Italy, where they overcame and settled Etruria and, in 390 B.C., sacked Rome itself. Others moved east into Asia Minor, attacking Delphi in 279 B.C.; a further wave moved east into Gaul and Britain. Despite regional differences, the Celts had in common their language, religion, and aristocratic warrior society, with heroic ideals and love of display (but also with admiration for learning and rhetoric). Contemporary classical writers describe them as fearless and 'madly fond of war.' They won great victories by physical strength, courage, and numbers, but lacked the political organization to plan campaigns. This made them ultimately vulnerable to the disciplined armies of Rome. A Roman victory at Telamon, Italy, in 225 B.C. was the beginning of their downfall, although it was not until 51 B.C. that Julius Caesar finally subjugated Gaul. Celtic traditions survived in the outposts of the British Isles. From there they would influence medieval art and literature, and would have a major impact upon the development of European Christianity.

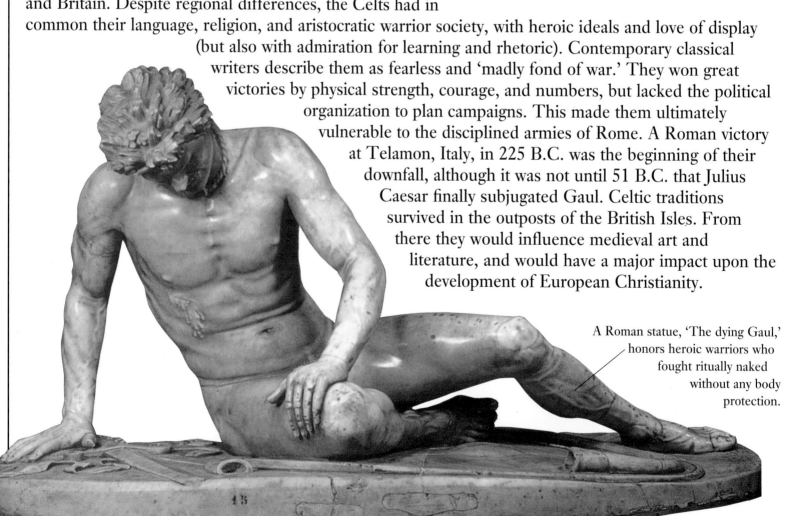

The Celtic aristocracy displayed wealth in the form of jewelry, with massive golden torcs (necklets; above). Warrior-queen Boudica (Boadicea) displayed such a 'great twisted golden necklace.'

A Roman statue, 'The dying Gaul,' honors heroic warriors who fought ritually naked without any body protection.

The sinuous snake motif is both ornament and sacred symbol. Snakes figure large in Celtic religion – perhaps the reason Christian St. Patrick exiled them from Ireland.

The wild boar, noted like Celtic warriors themselves for strength, ferocity, courage – and sexual prowess – was a sacred beast, strikingly portrayed in art.

Celts were great builders of forts, from family strongholds to walled towns. Hill forts were guarded by ditches and earthen banks (below, at Maiden Castle, Dorset, England), topped by ramparts of wood or stone.

FACT FILE

❏ La Tène art is one of the glories of the barbarian world. It combines linear patterns and sacred bird-shapes inherited from Bronze Age cultures with elements from trade contacts – Greek and Etruscan foliage designs; Scythian and Persian animal motifs. The resultant blend of naturalism and stylization was to inspire 19th century *Art Nouveau*.

❏ The Celts took great pride in their appearance. They valued a slim figure so highly that any youth too fat for the standard size belt was fined.

❏ Classical writers were struck by the Celts' flamboyance. They admired their courage, honor, and eloquence, but also recorded 'childish boastfulness and love of decoration' and 'vanity which makes them unbearable in victory and completely downcast in defeat.'

❏ Celtic warriors rode light, two-wheeled chariots (below) into battle. By driving into the heart of enemy forces, then leaping down to fight on foot, they combined, wrote Julius Caesar, 'the mobility of cavalry and the stability of infantry.'

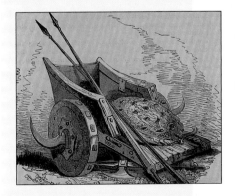

Four hundred forgotten gods

A fertility god carved from a chalk hillside, the Cerne Abbas Giant (Wiltshire, England) was believed to make barren women fertile until recent times.

'The whole Gaulish people [i.e., Celts],' noted Julius Caesar, 'is much given to religion.' They were indeed: the names of more than 400 Celtic deities survive. They remain mysterious, despite, or perhaps because of, a wealth of evidence, both archaeological and literary. The Celts revered the powers of nature and saw gods in natural objects – rivers, springs and wells, trees and groves. Naturally, this produced a multitude of regional and tribal gods and goddesses. The Romans tried to make sense of these by equating them with their own gods, but there was no formal pantheon like that of Rome. Celtic tribes probably shared a belief in a divine ancestor-god (later to become the Dagda, 'good god,' of Irish mythology) and an earth-goddess. Images of the horned god, the three-headed god, the god of the wheel, and the Triple Mothers recur across the Celtic world. The horned god, sometimes called Cernunnos, 'the Horned One,' is one of the best attested. His image survives in the horned Christian Devil – but before the coming of Christianity the antlered god was a divinity of peace and fertility. He often appears as 'lord of the beasts,' surrounded by the creations of Nature. Of course, the warlike Celts also revered a warrior god, who sometimes bears ram's or bull's horns. Regional war gods include Cocidius, recorded in Britain as 'god of soldiers,' and Camulos, equated in a Gaulish inscription with the Roman war god Mars. Goddesses were often threefold. The widespread cult of the Mothers, a triple goddess of fertility, is matched by a trinity of war-goddesses, the Morrigan.

'Lord of the beasts,' the god Cernunnos is antlered and attended by animals, including his particular emblems, a stag and, in his left hand, a ram-horned serpent. His right hand holds up a torc (necklet).

The god's cross-legged 'Buddhic' pose suggests oriental influence on Celtic cults. But classical writers record that the Celts squatted like this because they had not invented chairs.

An emblem of human sacrifice, the 'Monster of Noves' (France), rests its great claws on two severed heads while gnawing a human limb.

The severed human head was revered as a cult object, common in art – and in real life as a trophy of war. Enemy heads were mounted in temples or displayed at home, and skulls were made into gilded ritual drinking-cups.

FACT FILE

❏ The Celts held it improper to set down religious matters in writing. But oral traditions survived the introduction of Christianity, and the forgotten Celtic gods are still with us as the heroes of medieval Irish and Welsh mythological tales.

❏ Modern 'wishing wells' hark back to times when Celtic worshipers cast offerings into the sacred water of lakes, pools, rivers, wells, and bogs.

❏ After the Roman conquest, a Roman interpretation of Celtic gods became common. Many inscriptions equate a native deity with a Roman counterpart: e.g., north British war god Belatucadros is often identified with Roman war god Mars. So is the Celtic war god Teutates (familiar to modern children through the favorite oath of comic-strip hero 'Asterix the Gaul'). But basic differences are reflected in the inconsistency of equations: the horned god of the Brigantes is depicted variously as Mars, Mercury, and Silvanus.

❏ Pagan Celtic feast-days survived Christianity's coming. Imbolc (1 February), sacred to the goddess Brigit, became St Brigid's Day, and Lughnasad (1 August), sacred to sun god Lugh, became Lammas ('loaf-mass' – Harvest Festival); Samain (31 October), night of the dead, remains a sinister date in the Christian calendar – Hallowe'en – while the fertility ritual of Beltaine (1 May) survives as our May Day.

The Etruscans: Italian enigma

The Etruscans appeared in northern Italy in c.800 B.C. and soon dominated central Italy with a confederation of 12 independent city-states. Etruscan culture was so unlike that of neighboring peoples that its origins remain a mystery, although it seems to derive from a mixture of native Villanovans (Iron Age farmers) and Asian immigrants. Rich local mineral resources, efficient iron weapons, and extensive trade contacts with Greece and Phoenicia, made them a powerful economic and military force; a Roman historian said: 'Etruria filled the whole length of Italy with the noise of her name.' The Etruscans quickly acquired the technical expertise to build fine temples, roads, and well defended cities. Their art was sophisticated and distinctive, excelling in painting, sculpture, and metalwork. Their luxurious lifestyle – sumptuous banquets, rich furnishings, clothes and jewels, and a passion for music, dancing, and dice games – positively shocked the Greeks and Romans, who also disapproved of the freedom enjoyed by Etruscan women. But despite their differences, this wealthy, creative, and hedonistic culture contributed much to the formation of Rome, including its administrative framework, alphabet, 'century' system of organizing troops, gladiatorial games – and even its name. But Rome's rise was the downfall of the Etruscan city-states. In the 4th century B.C., lacking the political unity to stand together against a common enemy, they fell one by one to the Roman armies and became integrated into the Latin world.

Etruscan jewelry: delicate, intricate, and crowded with detail.

The helmet, more ceremonial than functional, copies its bonnet shape and lack of nosepiece from Greek models. It was probably crowned with upright feathers, Italian fashion.

Etruscan warrior. Etruscan military success was aided by borrowing Greek tactics, and relied on the use of hoplites – heavy infantry fighting in close packed formation.

Tiny gold balls soldered on a gold background sparkle with reflected light – a process not mastered again until this century.

Etruscan home territory lay in north Italy, between the Po and Arno Rivers. The city-states never united as a single empire, but at the height of its power the Etruscan world dominated northern and central Italy, with its influence extending westward into the island of Corsica.

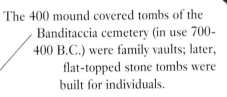

ALPS

Po River

Arno River

ETRURIA

Rome

APENNINES

TYRRHENIAN SEA

Etruscan power at its greatest extent c.540 B.C.

Wideset slanting eyes and the curved 'archaic smile' create an enigmatic calm. This terracotta head is all that remains of a lifesize statue of a warrior of the 5th century B,C.

The 400 mound covered tombs of the Banditaccia cemetery (in use 700-400 B.C.) were family vaults; later, flat-topped stone tombs were built for individuals.

FACT FILE

❏ Etruscan writing still baffles archaeologists. The script, a form of the Greek alphabet, presents no problems. The barrier is the language itself, unrelated to modern European languages and thought to have Stone Age roots. Only the simplest inscriptions have yielded so far to investigation.

❏ As early as 700 B.C., Etruscan dentists supplied false teeth of bone and ivory, with gold bridgework.

❏ Tombs form 'time capsules' of the Etruscan world, for the dead were equipped with all the comforts of life. Paintings and reliefs portray household furniture – comfortable beds, cooking utensils, weaponry, even slippers – as well as everyday activities. The dead themselves, modeled in terracotta on coffin lids (above), display fashionable clothing, hairstyles, jewelry, and elegant footwear.

❏ Etruscan engineers reclaimed large areas of wetland with underground drainage systems (*cuniculi*). They cut roads through hills, with gutters to prevent damage by flash floods. Some of these roads remain in use today.

City on seven hills

The city of Rome grew up on seven hills by the River Tiber, south Latium, Italy. Legend has it founded on April 21, 753 B.C., on the Palatine Hill, by Romulus and Remus, twin sons of the war-god Mars. Archaeological evidence too sets the site's first settlement in the 700s B.C., but ascribes it, less grandly, to Latin farmers who set up small villages of thatched huts. By the early 6th century, the villages on the seven hills had united to form a city. Nothing is known of the earliest kings of Rome, but in 616 B.C. an Etruscan with the Romanized name of Lucius Tarquinius took the throne and founded the Tarquin Dynasty. Lasting for more than a century, this had a profound influence on Roman culture. In 509 B.C., Rome expelled the last Tarquin ruler, Tarquinius Superbus ('the Proud'). The city rejected monarchy to become a republic, ruled by two consuls elected annually from the Senate, a group of wealthy noblemen. Soon afterwards, Rome joined the surrounding cities of Latium in the Latin League, a defensive alliance against neighboring tribes. Roman policy was now directed toward expansion, conquest, and consolidation. In 340 B.C. the other members of the Latin League resisted Rome's growing power, but within two years the Romans defeated their former allies and extended their control over Latium. Latin cities were either absorbed into the Roman state or granted self-government under Roman control. Meanwhile, the Romans were acquiring a knowledge of Greek civilization from Greek city-states in the south. By 260 B.C. Rome was both a major military power and a great civilization.

Temple of Jove

A reconstruction of the Forum, Rome's political and legal center. Major buildings included temples, triumphal arches, the Curia (Senate House), Basilica (Court House), the tomb of Romulus, and the Rostrum, or public speaking place.

Romulus and Remus, mythical founders of Rome, were said to have been left to die as babies, but saved by a wolf which suckled them with her cubs.

The legend that Romulus and Remus were suckled by a wolf may mean they were raised in a werewolf cult. The wolf was honored with a bronze statue in the 6th century B.C.: the figures of Romulus and Remus were not added until the Renaissance.

Temple of Saturn   Tabularium   Temple of Concorde

Temple of Vespasian   Navel of Rome   Julian Column   Arch of Septimus Severus

The Palatine Hill, site of Rome's first settlement, takes its name from Pales, god of shepherds, whose festival day of 21 April was traditionally the date when the city was founded.

FACT FILE

❏ Rome's equivalent of our 'A.D.' was 'A.U.C.' (*ab urbe condita*: 'from the foundation of the city', i.e., 753 B.C.).

❏ Legend says Romulus seized the women of the neighboring Sabines to provide wives for his men. Historically, the Sabines were assimilated into the early Roman population after a series of battles. Three of the six greatest families of the Roman republic claimed Sabine descent.

❏ Under the Tarquins, Etruscan engineers drained marshland for the site of the first Roman forum (above); laid the city's first sewer system (whose central channel, the *Cloaca Maxima*, survives); and raised temples and the first city walls. The Etruscan rulers also made the Capitoline Hill Rome's religious and political heart, as it is today.

Hannibal: hero from Africa

The North African city-state of Carthage controlled west Mediterranean trade routes from the 5th century B.C. Its attempts to colonize Sicily antagonized Rome. In the First Punic War (Romans called Carthaginians *peonicus*: 'dark skins'), 264-241, the landsmen of Rome defeated the seafaring state – at sea. Carthaginian galleys relied on ramming; the Romans countered with the *corvus*, a swivel-mounted boarding bridge that locked their ships to the enemy's, enabling 'marines' to storm across. At the outset of the Second Punic War (218-201), the Carthaginian general Hannibal (247-182 B.C.) boldly decided to carry the war to Italy. With an army including squadrons of elephants, he marched from southern Spain, over the Pyrenees, and across Gaul; then led his men and beasts in an amazing 15-day transit of the snowy Alps. In Italy his mercenary army (native Carthaginians saw themselves as seamen, not soldiers) shattered Roman legions by ambush at Lake Trasimene (217) and by encirclement at Cannae (216), where Rome lost c.50,000 men; Hannibal only 8,000. But Rome's allies did not desert to him as he had hoped: he held much of Italy for some 10 years, but his forces were worn down by Roman delaying tactics. Carthage called him home to face a Roman counter-invasion in 204, and in 202, after his defeat at Zama, banished him. In the Third Punic War (149-146 B.C.), Scipio Africanus the Younger (185-129 B.C.) took Carthage by siege, leveled the city, and symbolically sowed salt on its ruins. But Carthage rose again – as a prosperous Roman colony from c.50 B.C. to A.D. 697, when it was finally destroyed by the Arabs.

A carving from the site of Carthage, in modern Tunisia, shows an elephant in action. Although Hannibal showed ingenuity in rafting elephants over the Rhone and marching them across the Alps, they had small part in his victories.

Unlike Alexander the Great, whose elephants came from India, Hannibal used comparatively small African forest elephants, which then lived in the wild in Morocco and Tunisia.

Hannibal's route in the Second Punic War. He marched from Cartagena (New Carthage) across Spain and Gaul, won great battles in Italy, but was called home to face defeat at Zama (modern Jama).

This Carthaginian figure dates from the Roman period of the early centuries A.D. The Romans thoroughly destroyed the ancient city soon after c.146 B.C.

Peaceful activities feature on a stone tablet from Roman Carthage, c.1st century A.D.

Scenes of animal husbandry reflect Carthage's change from Rome's enemy to its prosperous commercial colony.

❑ Hannibal's elephants were probably more use as beasts of burden than fighting machines. Elephants could break up cavalry forces – their size, smell, and sound, stampeded horses – but determined spearmen who faced them found that even slight wounds made them flee, trampling friendly troops to their rear, or run amok as a danger to friend and foe alike.

❑ Hannibal's Italian campaign was defeated by Fabius Maximus (d.203 B.C.). Because Fabius refused to seek pitched battles, his countrymen mocked him as '*Cunctator*' ('Delayer'). But his careful maneuvers fatally weakened Hannibal's force (which got little help from Carthage), and the nickname became Fabius's title of honor.

❑ Hannibal's last 20 years were spent as a mercenary in Asia Minor. Rome's vengeance pursued him always, and in 182, when Rome demanded his extradition from Syria, he killed himself.

❑ Roman statesman Marcus Porcius Cato 'the Elder' (c.234-149 B.C.), who had served as a legionary officer during the Second Punic War, became Carthage's most bitter enemy. Before the Third Punic War, he ended every speech he made in the Senate, whatever its subject, with the dire warning '*Delenda est Carthago*' ('Carthage must be destroyed').

Caesar: Colossus of Rome

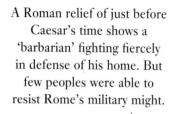

A Roman relief of just before Caesar's time shows a 'barbarian' fighting fiercely in defense of his home. But few peoples were able to resist Rome's military might.

'He doth bestride the narrow world like a Colossus.' Shakespeare's description is simple truth: there was no more remarkable Roman than Gaius Julius Caesar (100-44 B.C.), supreme as general and politician, matched by few as orator and author. Although a patrician (nobleman), he achieved political power as spokesman of the plebeians (commoners), and by 60 B.C. was, with Gnaeus Pompeius Magnus ('Pompey the Great') (106-48 B.C.) and Marcus Licinius Crassus, one of a ruling 'Triumvirate.' Pompey and Caesar vied for military glory: Pompey in the east, bringing Palestine and Syria under Roman rule; Caesar in the west, with his conquest of Gaul (58-51) and two invasions of Britain (55-54). After Crassus's death, Pompey's supporters, dominant in Rome itself, planned to make their man sole ruler. Caesar was ordered to leave his armies and return to Rome to face political, and probably literal, death. Instead, in January 49, he led his veteran legions, who would have followed their charismatic general to Hades (Hell), across the Rubicon River (border between Gaul and Italy) towards Rome. Pompey retreated to northern Greece, where he was defeated at Pharsalus (48); then fled to Egypt, where he was murdered. Caesar became absolute ruler, and generally acted wisely and fairly. But his behavior was increasingly 'kingly,' and by February 44, when he took the title 'dictator for life,' many of his former supporters believed he intended to destroy the Republic. On the Ides (15th day) of March 44, 23 dagger thrusts by conspirators led by Marcus Junius Brutus (c.85-42 B.C.) and Gaius Cassius Longinus (d.42 B.C.) brought down the Colossus.

Vercingetorix (executed by the Romans, 46 B.C.) led Gaulish resistance to Caesar's conquest. This heroic statue at Alise-Sainte-Reine (Alesia) was erected in 1865 to mark the site of his final defeat, 52 B.C.

These remains of a Gallo-Roman settlement are on the hill top at Alesia, east central France, where c.100,000 Gauls under Vercingetorix were besieged by Caesar's legions.

Julius Caesar's proud boast was: *'Veni, vidi, vici'* ('I came, I saw, I conquered'). Although he was not a professional soldier – he did not command an army until he was in his forties – he was one of history's greatest generals.

Typical of Roman public statuary, this figure shows Caesar stiffly posed in the attitude of a statesman delivering a speech. Statues showing dignitaries in armor, like this, were called *loricatae*; in civilian dress, they were *togatae*.

FACT FILE

❏ The professional army that helped Caesar to power owed much to reforms made by Gaius Marius (157-86 B.C.). He widened the legions' recruiting base; reorganized tactical formations like the 'cohort' (500-600 men; divided into six 'centuries'); and standardized legionaries' equipment. His soldiers, each required to carry arms, armor, and gear together weighing c.80-100lb (35-44kg), called themselves 'Marius's Mules.' The typical legion thereafter consisted of 10 cohorts (c. 6,000 men). Each had its own name, number, and *aquila* (eagle standard).

❏ The legionary's principal weapons were the *gladius*, a short, straight, two-edged sword; *pilum*, a c.6ft (1.8m) spear; and *scutum*, a 4ft (1.2m) tall shield of layered leather or wood up to 0.75in (19mm) thick. Shod with the *caligula*, a hob-nailed sandal, a legion might march 15mi (24km) or more in a day – and then build a fortified camp before resting.

❏ Marcus Licinius Crassus (c.155-53 B.C.) achieved power through his immense wealth and his suppression of the Italian slave revolt led by Spartacus. Seeking military glory to rival Caesar and Pompey, he led an invasion of Parthia, where his legions were annihilated at the battle of Carrhae, 53 B.C. It is said the Parthians filled the mouth of his severed head with molten gold as a comment on his notorious greed.

Antony, Augustus – and Empire

This commanding image of Emperor Augustus as 'father of his people' dates from around his own life time. His cuirass (breast plate) shows scenes from a victory over Parthians.

Caesar's death in 44 B.C. gave rise to civil war between the republicans led by Brutus and Cassius, and Caesar's followers, headed by Marcus Antonius (Mark Antony) (83-30 B.C.). In 43, Antony, a good but reckless general, Marcus Aemilius Lepidus (d.13 B.C.), a wealthy politician, and young Gaius Octavius (Octavian) (63 B.C.-A.D. 14), Caesar's nephew and adopted heir, formed the 'Second Triumvirate.' Antony and Octavian defeated the republicans, whose leaders committed suicide, at Philippi in 42, and agreed to divide Rome's territories. Antony took the east, where he became the lover of Caesar's former mistress, Queen Cleopatra VII of Egypt. Octavian's distrust came to a head in 36-34, when Antony first wed Cleopatra (in spite of his existing, politically dictated, marriage to Octavian's sister), then declared her son Caesarion (supposedly fathered by Caesar) rightful heir to Rome. A new civil war ended with the defeat of Antony and Cleopatra at the naval battle of Actium (31 B.C.). Both committed suicide – Cleopatra probably only after finding she could not seduce Octavian as she had Caesar and Antony. Having pacified Asia, Octavian returned to Rome in triumph in 29, and in 28 assumed supreme rule as *'Imperator Caesar Augustus'* (all three titles became a synonym for 'Emperor'). Augustus ('Most Revered'), as Octavian was thereafter known, was the first and greatest Roman emperor. During the long 'Augustan Age,' the Empire's frontiers were expanded and strengthened; trade flourished; and Roman culture reached its height. It was said of his patronage of the arts that 'he found Rome brick, and left it marble.'

The statue was made for Prima Porta, villa of Augustus's wife Livia Drusilla (58 B.C.-A.D.29), whom some say was a 'power behind the throne.'

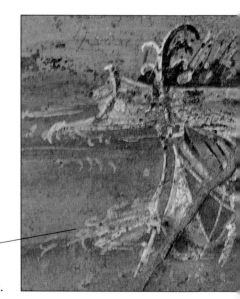

At the battle of Actium, Augustus deployed fast, light war galleys (*liburnae*) like these, packed with soldiers, to defeat Antony's larger, slower quinqueremes.

In 30 B.C. Augustus added Alexandria to the Roman Empire. This column in the city, 'Pompey's Pillar,' is said to mark the tomb of the general defeated by Julius Caesar – but was built to honor Emperor Diocletian (A.D. 245-313).

The Romans made 'death masks' in wax of prominent persons – and this image of Mark Antony may be from such a source. He avenged the murder of his patron Julius Caesar; then became the lover of Caesar's former mistress Cleopatra. He committed suicide after being defeated by Augustus.

Above the strengthened projection of the ram at the galley's prow is an 'eye,' supposed to guide it on its way.

FACT FILE

❏ In Caesar's time, '*Imperator*' was a title given as an honor to generals who won great battles. His immediate successors preferred the title 'Caesar,' in honor of the great man (from it stem the Russian and German titles, *Tsar* and *Kaiser*.) Later, the Roman ruler was usually called 'Emperor,' and his heir was known as 'Caesar.'

❏ Cleopatra (above) had a 'bad press' from early historians – one claimed she had had 10,000 lovers – probably because she was a shrewd, ruthless power seeker at a time when women were expected to be political pawns. At various times she was married to two of her brothers (as Egyptian royal custom dictated), and bore Caesarion (perhaps by Caesar) and twins, Alexander Helios and Cleopatra Selene, by Antony. Her sons were murdered at Octavian's command; Cleopatra Selene became queen of Numidia.

Roman gods and men

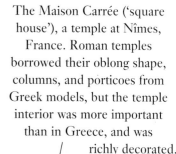

The Maison Carrée ('square house'), a temple at Nîmes, France. Roman temples borrowed their oblong shape, columns, and porticoes from Greek models, but the temple interior was more important than in Greece, and was richly decorated.

Roman religion borrowed from several nations, but was based on that of Greece. The chief gods were seen as a family of immortals, with many mortal characteristics. They were essentially the Greek gods under different names: Greek Zeus became Roman Jupiter; Hera became Juno; Ares became Mars; Aphrodite became Venus; Athene became Minerva. Alongside these gods of the state religion, hundreds of local demi-gods and spirits were worshiped. Every household honored its guardian spirits, the *lares* and *penates*; each individual had his own protective spirit, or *genius*. Religious tolerance extended to the worship of foreign gods: the Egyptian goddess Isis and the Persian god Mithras were among the most popular. The gods were appeased with sacrifices: the head of each household made offerings to the gods on behalf of his family; the Emperor acted as high priest (*Pontifex Maximus*) on behalf of Rome itself. Under the Caesars this led to the actual deification of the emperor. Most were declared gods after their deaths – although the insane Caligula (ruled A.D. 37-41) deified himself – and, like other gods, had magnificent temples and images raised to them. But Rome's immense building and engineering skills were also employed for more practical purposes. Many Roman roads and bridges, built to speed the passage of marching legions, are still in use (albeit after much repair), and not until the late A.D. 1700s could Western civilization match such works of civil engineering as the great aqueducts built to bring water to the Empire's cities.

The *lar* guarded the home, along with *penates* (larder spirits) and Vesta, goddess of the hearth. *Lares* began as protectors of farmland; when urban growth began they moved with the times, and became guardian spirits of the cities.

The pagan cult to stand longest against the Christianity of the later Empire was probably that of Mithras (right), originally Persian god of light. It was enthusiastically adopted by soldiers, for whom it constituted a 'secret society' much like modern Freemasonry.

By slaying the sacred bull the god creates life: the Mithraic mystery.

Apollo, sun god and patron of the arts, was a Greek deity who was worshiped in Rome before 432 B.C.

❑ The deification of the emperor was taken seriously, but for political rather than religious reasons. By insisting that an emperor's image take pride of place in all temples, the Romans emphasized their superiority over subject peoples. Emperor Claudius (10 B.C.-A.D. 54) is said to have joked on his death bed (presumably not knowing he was dying of poison given by his wife and servants): 'I seem to be turning into a god!'

❑ Roman religious tolerance did not extend to Judaism or, until the 2nd-3rd centuries A.D., to Christianity. Both religions held that there was only one god, and thus denied the divinity of the emperor. Both were savagely persecuted.

❑ The longest Roman aqueduct was the Aqueduct of Carthage, Tunisia, which ran 87.6mi (141km) from the wells of Zaghouan to Djebel Djougar. It was built in A.D. 117-138, and had an original capacity calculated at 7,000,000gal (26,495,000l) per day.

❑ A Roman could call upon the gods for revenge on an enemy by writing a curse on a sheet of lead at a temple or local shrine. Many examples survive; one prays: 'May he who carried off Vilbia from me become as liquid as water,' and lists suspects by name. Another curses an enemy's 'life and mind and memory and liver and lungs mixed up together.'

Pompeii: buried city

On August 24-27, A.D. 79, the volcano Vesuvius erupted, destroying several towns around the Bay of Naples. The prosperous city of Pompeii, with some 2,000 of its c.15-20,000 inhabitants, was buried under c.13ft (4m) of volcanic debris. It lay hidden until its ruins were discovered in the 16th century. Excavation, begun in the 18th century and still continuing, revealed the pattern of everyday life in a Roman city. The survivors of Pompeii's destruction, fleeing gas clouds, storms of ash, and rivers of molten lava, departed in such haste that they left meals on their tables, loaves baking in their ovens, and unfinished drinks on bar counters. More than half the city has now been uncovered, revealing not only the straight, stone paved streets, fine public buildings, and comfortable villas that we generally associate with the Romans, but the less familiar tenement rooms of the poor, and the many shops, taverns, and factories of a busy trading center. In the villas, mosaic floors and wall-paintings in grand public rooms contrast with more intimate aspects of life: the kitchen, with oven, sink, and cooking pots; the somewhat insanitary lavatory under the stairs. The tradesmen's world, too, is on display: hardware merchants' and bronzesmiths' premises, textile workshops, and food shops. Wall paintings show how wares were made and marketed. The city's facilities included three large public baths, an amphitheater for games – and two theaters, where the names of crowd-pullers of 1,900 years ago still appear on the walls: 'Actius, darling of the people;' 'Paris, pearl of the stage.'

Apollo's statue still adorns its pedestal in the temple court. Poised in flight, his arms stretch to launch an arrow from his bow, now missing.

Mount Vesuvius looms beyond the Temple of Apollo, Pompeii. An eruption in A.D. 62 wrecked Pompeii, which was rebuilt in even greater splendor – and completely destroyed only 17 years later.

Ashes and pumice covered the dead of Pompeii, and then hardened, forming casts of the bodies. When clothes and flesh decayed, their details remained imprinted in these casts.

Many fell in terrified flight, some striving to save goods. Temple treasures weighed down devoted priests; one man lost his life trying to rescue an awkward goat.

A large bread oven at one of Pompeii's 20 bakeries. Fleeing bakers left bread in the ovens – round flat loaves, often stamped with the bakery's trademark.

The baker ground his own flour between millstones of grey lava. The mill was turned by a donkey – in some cases by slaves.

Herculaneum was spared the crushing weight of lava: many houses remain intact with top stories and roofs.

Walls built of rubble and cement were decorated with a network pattern of square stones in diagonal rows.

Herculaneum was a quiet provincial city, as its streets show, lacking Pompeii's deep ruts cut by heavy traffic.

❏ The naturalist Pliny the Elder, at sea near Pompeii when Vesuvius erupted, led a rescue mission across the Bay of Naples. Unable to land near the doomed city, he lost his life in the attempt, succumbing to poisonous fumes. His nephew, Pliny the Younger, left an eye-witness account of the disaster, describing the threatening cloud, 'like a huge pine tree,' that rose from Vesuvius.

❏ No wooden items survived under the volcanic ash at Pompeii. But nearby Herculaneum was buried under c.43ft (13m) of boiling mud, which preserved many wooden objects in carbonated form. These range from beds and tables to a household shrine and a baby's cot with rockers.

❏ The walls of Pompeii bear finely lettered advertisements and election slogans – as well as graffiti such as: 'Do not relieve yourself here: the stinging nettles are long!'

❏ The earliest example of 'loaded' dice was found at Pompeii, the Roman city swamped by the eruption of Vesuvius.

❏ One Pompeiian villa contains a white marble table on which is carved the name of P. Casca Longus – a name known to us as one of Julius Caesar's assassins in 44 B.C. Perhaps some of Casca's confiscated property found its way to Pompeii.

Bread and circuses

Around A.D. 1, the population of the city of Rome approached one million. With most manual labor done by slaves, there was little employment for many thousand unskilled but free citizens who crowded the city's tenements (as many as 11 or 12 rickety stories). To win the political support of this 'mob,' politicians – from emperors to ward heelers – favored a policy summed up by the poet Juvenal (A.D. 60-130) as '*panem et circenses*' ('bread, and circus games'). 'Bread' was the public dole, for all unemployed citizens; 'games' were chariot racing, wild beast shows, and gladiatorial fights. Chariot racing centered on the Circus Maximus, where up to 12 four-horse chariots (representing four 'colors,' supported like today's pro football teams) fought it out over seven laps of a 660yd (600m) track before up to 250,000 spectators. Betting, and the prospect of spectacular crashes at the track's two sharp curves, were the main attractions. At wild beast shows, animals fought in cross-species combat (lion versus bull was a favorite); were killed by 'hunters'; or were starved, enraged, and let loose to slaughter war captives or condemned criminals. In gladiatorial shows, specially trained fighting men (usually slaves or criminals) met in single combat or melee. Huge sums changed hands as patrons wagered whether a fast-moving *retiarus* (unarmored, with net and trident) or *thracian* (small round shield, curved dagger) would win out over a slower, well armored *murmillo* (swordsman) or *samnite* (short sword or ax). Fights were often to the death, although a defeated man who had fought well might be spared by the crowd's acclaim.

Magnificent in ruins, the Colosseum is a glory to modern as it was to ancient Rome. It was so well designed that 50,000 people could be admitted, seated, or cleared from the stadium, in minutes.

Lightly armed men, probably war captives or condemned criminals, fight with wild beasts to entertain the Roman mob.

Animals were brought from all over the Empire to die in the 'games.' Big cats, bears, rhinos, and crocodiles were among beasts set against humans or each other.

❑ Delight in spectacular bloodshed reached its height in the Colosseum (Amphitheatrum Flavium), with seating for c.50,000 people. Its opening by Emperor Titus in A.D. 80 was marked by 100 days of games in which c.9,000 animals were killed, and hundreds of gladiators (above) died. The arena could be flooded for mock sea battles.

❑ Contrary to popular belief, there is no reliable record of Christians ever being thrown to wild beasts in the Colosseum, though they may have been martyred in this way in other stadia, erected all over the Roman world.

Now visible beneath the arena is a network of cells and passages from which men and beasts were brought up in elevators and appeared through trap doors.

Most chariot drivers began as slaves. A lucky few might win both freedom and wealth.

It took immense skill and cold courage to drive a four-horse racing chariot. Spectacular crashes pleased the crowds.

The westward course of Empire

All over the Empire, grand edifices testified to the power of Rome.

This massive arch was built at Volubilis (in modern Morocco, then a Roman province) to mark the death of Emperor Caracalla in A.D. 217.

Emperor Augustus set out to rationalize the Empire. He divided Gaul and Spain into three provinces each, and from 12 B.C. tried to expand Rome's German frontier to the Elbe River. In A.D. 9, resisting Roman expansion, German armies led by the Cheruscan chief Arminius (Hermann) destroyed three legions at the Battle of Teutoburger Wald, driving the Romans back to the Rhine frontier. Further Roman expeditions failed to defeat Arminius, and Germany remained free. In Britain, too, tribes rose against Rome. In A.D. 61, Boudica, queen of the powerful Iceni, protested the harsh taxation of Roman governor Suetonius Paulinus. She was flogged, her daughters raped, and her palace sacked. The Romans had underestimated the power of a Celtic queen. Boudica led the tribes of eastern Britain in revolt. They stormed the Roman settlement at Camulodunum (Colchester), burned the town, massacred its inhabitants, and destroyed the IX Legion. Boudica went on to sack Verulamium (St Albans) and Londinium (London). At last Suetonius routed the British and took a savage revenge. Boudica committed suicide, but Suetonius was dismissed for excessive harshness and, following Emperor Claudius's conquest in A.D. 43, Britain settled down as a Roman province. Under the *Pax Romana* ('Roman peace') military rule gave way to local government involving native peoples. New legal and monetary systems, and better communications, encouraged trade and industry. Prosperous Britons had a Roman lifestyle, with comfortable town houses or country villas. Native arts were not destroyed, but contributed to a sophisticated Romano-British culture.

Statues line the bath house at Bath, England. Public baths, a mark of Roman civilization, were among the Empire's finest buildings.

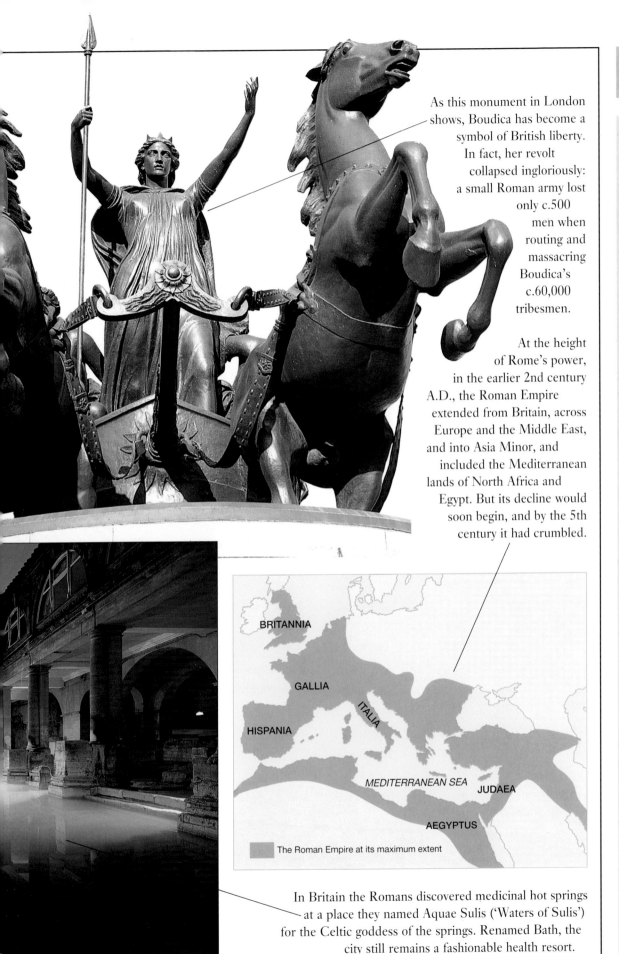

As this monument in London shows, Boudica has become a symbol of British liberty. In fact, her revolt collapsed ingloriously: a small Roman army lost only c.500 men when routing and massacring Boudica's c.60,000 tribesmen.

At the height of Rome's power, in the earlier 2nd century A.D., the Roman Empire extended from Britain, across Europe and the Middle East, and into Asia Minor, and included the Mediterranean lands of North Africa and Egypt. But its decline would soon begin, and by the 5th century it had crumbled.

BRITANNIA

GALLIA

ITALIA

HISPANIA

MEDITERRANEAN SEA

JUDAEA

AEGYPTUS

■ The Roman Empire at its maximum extent

In Britain the Romans discovered medicinal hot springs at a place they named Aquae Sulis ('Waters of Sulis') for the Celtic goddess of the springs. Renamed Bath, the city still remains a fashionable health resort.

❏ Publius Quinctilius Varus, Roman commander during Arminius's rebellion, lost c.18,000 legionaries and 1,500 cavalry in the forest ambush of Teutoburger Wald. Varus escaped capture by suicide, but the Germans took his head and the legions' eagle standards as trophies. Augustus is said to have wept: 'Varus, Varus, give me back my legions!' Varus's three legions were never re-formed, but the eagles were recovered over the next century. Arminius, himself a Roman citizen and former officer of auxiliaries, was assassinated by his own people when he tried to make himself king over them in A.D.19.

❏ Boudica's name – from Celtic *bouda* ('victory') – translates literally and appropriately as 'Victoria.' The earlier spelling 'Boadicea' was a medieval scribe's error.

❏ The first towns of Roman Britain were built at tribal centers, to bring urban culture to the native aristocracy. Other towns were *coloniae*, settlements where veteran legionaries were given property grants as 'pensions.'

❏ Roman rule in Britain endured until A.D. 410 – when many Britons lamented the 'flight of the eagles,' as the legions withdrew to defend Rome itself. Sea raiders from Europe, Ireland, and Scandinavia moved in and laid waste to Roman Britain.

On the Wall

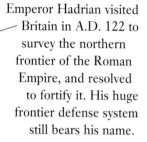

Gnaeus Julius Agricola, governor of Britain in A.D. 78-84, extended Roman rule north into Scotland as far as the Forth and Clyde Rivers. But after defeating the Scots at the battle of Mons Graupius (83), he called a halt, leaving the Highlands unconquered. By c.100 the Picts and other Scots tribes had recovered from their defeat. They attacked the northern forts and from c.117 raided into northern England. Soon their threat was such that Emperor Hadrian (ruled 117-138) himself came from Rome to investigate. He decided against an expensive war, choosing instead to 'separate the Romans and the barbarians' with country-wide defensive works. 'Hadrian's Wall' ran some 75mi (120km) from coast to coast. It was built in c.122-128 by legionaries, whose basic training included the building of fortifications – although not often on such a huge scale. Built largely of stone and with deep ditches on either side, the Wall was some 15ft (4.6m) high and up to 10ft (3m) wide, with battlements, a sentry walk along the top, and forts at regular intervals. It was served by a road on the south side, and garrisoned by c.14,000 soldiers – about one third of Roman military strength in Britain. For some 250 years the Wall held back the Scots: it was stormed by tribesmen in the late 190s and partially demolished, but was restored to its full strength under Emperor Septimus Severus (ruled 193-211). In the late 4th century, when the Roman withdrawal from Britain began, the Wall was abandoned. Today, its ruins are among the greatest monuments of Roman Britain.

Emperor Hadrian visited Britain in A.D. 122 to survey the northern frontier of the Roman Empire, and resolved to fortify it. His huge frontier defense system still bears his name.

Hadrian's Wall was not a defense line held by soldiers from behind, but a well-planned attack base, a frontier patrol track, and, perhaps above all, a symbol of the dominion of Rome.

The soldiers who built this wall also quarried the stone. Carved graffiti in the quarries tell their side of the story: 'Stadius did this,' and, 'I, Daminius, did not want to do it.'

In many places the Wall runs along steep crags, making a defensive ditch unnecessary, as here, near Housesteads Fort.

Reconstructed milecastle-gateway at Vindolanda, where a Roman fort guarded the northern frontier before the Wall was built.

❑ Hadrian's Wall had 16 major forts (e.g. Housesteads, below) at 5mi (8km) intervals, each holding a cohort (500 men). 80 'milecastles,' at intervals of a Roman mile (c.1620yd/1480m), each housed 100 men.

❑ Between the wall and its service road to the south lay the *Vallum*, an 'exclusion zone' consisting of a ditch some 20ft (6m) wide at the top and c.10ft (3m) deep. Flanked by high mounds, it made an obstacle some 120ft (37m) wide, crossed only by causeways opposite the forts.

❑ After Hadrian's death, Roman forces advanced north of the Wall. In c.140, in the reign of Emperor Antoninus Pius, they began a second frontier wall to contain their new territory. The 'Antonine Wall' was a barrier of turf c.37mi (60km) long, garrisoned by c.7,000 men. In c.180, a rising of the Highland tribes forced the Romans to abandon their new frontier and retreat to Hadrian's Wall.

❑ Hadrian's Wall is rich in Roman graffiti – much like modern soldiers' inscriptions: 'Lucius was here'; 'Our centurion is a ****'; 'British weather sucks!'

Decline and fall

Rome's decline accelerated after the death of Emperor Marcus Aurelius in A.D.180. His heir, Commodus, was murdered in 193, and a succession of generals seized power. Between 210 and 284, when Diocletian took the throne, there were 27 emperors – 23 of whom were murdered. None had time for the duties of government. Taxation soared; trade declined; barbarians took advantage of Rome's civil wars to press harder on the frontiers. Diocletian adopted the desperate remedy of dividing an Empire too stressed to unite under a single ruler. He ruled in the East, giving the West to a co-Emperor, Maximian – but peace did not long outlast his death. In 323 the Eastern Emperor Constantine I defeated the Western Emperor Licinius and united the Empire once more. He made Christianity its official religion and moved his capital to Byzantium, renamed Constantinople. But his successors were unable to maintain a single Empire, and the division became final on the death of Theodosius in 395. The Eastern Empire prospered, but the West was assailed by barbarian tribes, some of whom it was forced to take into military alliance and allow to settle within its borders. In 409, the sack of Rome itself by Goths led by Alaric was of small political significance – Emperor Honorius's government was safe in the fortified city of Ravenna – but the damage to Rome's prestige was enormous. The disintegration of the Western Empire soon followed. Its last emperor, Romulus Augustulus, a puppet of the barbarians, was deposed in 476 by the Gothic general Odoacer, and the Western Empire gave way to barbarian kingdoms.

A gold coin of Emperor Valentinian I (reigned A.D. 364-75) shows Roman arms triumphant – an increasingly rare event at that time.

Praetorian Guardsmen are identified as officers by the ornate horsehair crests on their helmets.

From the time of Augustus, soldiers of the elite Praetorian Guard, normally between 9-15,000 strong, were the emperors' body guard – and as such a political power.

This column was erected in Rome to mark the reign (161-80) of Emperor Marcus Aurelius, philosopher and soldier. Its carvings concentrate on his military exploits.

Legionaries round up prisoners. Scenes like these featured in Marcus's campaigns that temporarily halted a Parthian invasion of Syria, in the east, and stemmed an invasion of Italy by Germanic 'barbarians.'

A huge carving in modern Iran marks Roman humiliation: captured while battling a Persian invasion, Emperor Valerian (reigned A.D. 253-60) is forced to kneel to King Shapur I.

FACT FILE

❏ Rome's decline was probably speeded by health problems. Romans suffered lead-poisoning from the pipes carrying the city's water supply, and were enervated by malaria. For 500 years, Rome's population was chronically infected with this disease, called 'Roman airs.' Many moralistic 19th century historians pointed to sexual licence – in particular an increase in toleration of homosexuality – as a reason for Rome's decline.

❏ Emperor Constantine I (c.274-337) hoped Christianity would help unify the Empire. Although himself not 'officially' a Christian, he claimed to have been assured of victory in a crucial battle at the Milvian Bridge, near Rome, in 312, by a vision of the sign of the cross with the words 'In hoc vinces' ('In this [sign] conquer'). In 313 he proclaimed toleration and recognition of Christianity throughout the Empire.

❏ The most able defender of Italy against the Goths, Flavius Stilicho (c.359-408), was himself a 'barbarian,' a Vandal, but was related by marriage to the Emperors Theodosius and Honorius. In 403-406 he defeated Gothic armies up to 400,000 strong in northern Italy. But when he suggested an alliance with the Gothic leader, Alaric, against the Vandals, his own people, and the Alans, who were overrunning Gaul, Honorius had him murdered.

Attila: 'Scourge of God'

This iron Avar (Hunnish) stirrup dates from the 8th century A.D. Authorities are divided as to whether this device, invaluable to the mounted warrior, was known as early as Attila's time.

From the 1st century A.D. the Huns, Mongoloid warriors of the central Asian steppe, moved west on their shaggy ponies. Their migration drove Ostrogoths and Visigoths from southern Russia and the Balkans into Roman territory, contributing to the destabilization of the Empire. By the 4th century, the Huns were running a lucrative 'protection racket' from Hungary, raiding south and west, then accepting huge bribes to withdraw; others served as mercenaries with Roman or barbarian armies. In c.434, Hun kingship passed to the brothers Bleda and Attila (c.406-453); by c.445 Attila had murdered Bleda and, by threats and sheer force of personality, united the Hunnish chiefs under his leadership. Claiming the Romans had broken treaties, he led his riders across the Danube, ravaging the Roman Empire to the gates of Constantinople, then turned west. He demanded Honoria, sister of Western Emperor Valentinian III, for his wife – with all Gaul as her bridal gift. Valentinian refused: Attila invaded Gaul. Romans and barbarians united against the threat: in 451, on the Catalaunian Plains (near Chalôns-sur-Marne, or Troyes, France) Roman general Aetius and Visigothic King Theodoric (killed in action) defeated Attila in a day-long, bloody battle. In 452 Attila rode into Italy, devastating the prosperous Po Valley. Pope Leo I somehow persuaded him to withdraw. It was claimed the Pope's 'holiness' overawed the militant pagan whom Christians called the 'Scourge of God;' more likely, Attila's force was too weak, from battle loss and plague, to continue. Following his death the next year, his Hunnish federation disintegrated.

The Mausoleum of Theodoric, Ostrogothic ruler of Italy in 493-526, at Ravenna. The crumbling Roman Empire's western capital had moved north from Rome to Ravenna in 402.

Note the prominence of the stirrup on this Arab coin of c.A.D. 900. Some writers ascribe Attila's victories to its use, which gave mounted archers a steady aiming seat.

A romantic artist's view of Attila lacks truth. Huns, shown near naked, were noted for love of finery, gold and jewels – and they were mounted archers, not swordsmen on foot.

This part at least of the artist's vision is credible: innocent civilians lie slaughtered on the path of Attila's ruthless raiders.

❏ The Huns were said to 'live on horseback,' eating, sleeping (and, some said, mating) without dismounting. Their primary weapon was the composite bow; their greatest appetites for gold and good horses (the Roman 'heavy horse' was one of the lures that drew them west). Their appearance, with faces disfigured by ritual scars, contributed to Western legends that they were semi-demons.

❏ According to contemporary writers, Attila was a near dwarf (perhaps 4ft 2in/1.3m tall) and extremely ugly. His death, it is recorded, was as bloody as his life: over exerting himself with a new addition to his harem of wives, he brought on a nose-bleed and choked to death on his own blood. Much later, as 'Atli,' he became one of the heroes of the great Germanic epic, the *Nibelungenlied*.

❏ The victory of Flavius Aetius (d.454) on the Catalaunian Plains was due partly to his close knowledge of his enemy. He had been a Hunnish hostage, had commanded Hunnish mercenaries, and was said to be a personal friend of Attila. He might have wiped out the Hunnish horde completely, but feared that after such a complete victory the Visigoths, his temporary allies, might turn on him. In 454, claiming that Aetius planned to dethrone him, Emperor Valentinian personally stabbed the general to death.

SUPERFACTS

Flint factories ▼
Some 2.5 million years ago, Stone Age flint knappers in Ethiopia formed communities dedicated to chipping out cutting tools and hand axes – the first 'industry' on record. Their craft included repair jobs, like shaping a new cutting edge on a blunted axe. A whetstone used to give tools a final polish is shown below.

First farmers ▼
Farming began when people first cultivated food plants instead of relying on natural growth. There is evidence of cultivation in Thailand as early as 11,000 B.C. Later, men supplemented hunting by taming food animals. The first species domesticated, probably c.8500 B.C., were sheep and goats. Cattle and pigs followed. Below: cattle of ancient Egypt, painted on the walls of a queen's tomb.

Fashionable fabrics
Textiles were discovered in the Stone Age. Woolen fabric from Catal Hüyük, Turkey, used for clothing, and probably also for rugs and hangings, has been dated to 5900 B.C. Fabrics made from plant fibers have an even longer history, and were known in Mesoamerica more than 10,000 years ago. Linen was woven in Egypt by c.4000 B.C., and cotton cloth in India by c.3000 B.C.

Stone Age scripts
Archaeologists long believed that ancient European civilizations did not develop writing independently. Modern researchers are not so sure. A site at Tartaria (Transylvania) yielded three clay tablets with incised marks, suggesting that Late Stone

Age people there invented a script which later fell into disuse. An incised stone from the Late Stone Age village of Skara Brae (Orkney, Scotland) possibly also represents a locally developed form of notation.

Watering the fields
Many ancient civilizations depended on irrigation to bring water and fertility to naturally arid land. Methods ranged from simple ditches, filled from wells and rivers, to vast complexes of canals, dams, and reservoirs. The oldest known canals, near Mandali, Iraq, date back to c.4000 B.C.

Jaguar children
Olmec artists of c.1200-500 B.C. depicted the 'were-jaguar,' a figure combining the features of a jaguar and a human child. Some researchers see it as a stylized representation of a child with congenital skull deformities caused by spina bifida. It is possible that such children were born to the ruling family – who chose to regard them as evidence of their descent from the sacred jaguar itself.

Master builders ▲
Stone Age engineering skills created an elaborate passage grave at Newgrange, County Meath, Ireland (c.2500 B.C.). A vast cairn covered a burial chamber and 60ft (18.3m) long entrance passage, built of more than 300 glacial boulders. The chamber, 20ft (6m) high, is roofed by overhanging slabs, positioned so accurately that they remain in perfect balance without mortar. A hidden 'window' in the roof allows the sun's rays to enter at dawn on Midwinter Day. Similar mathematical precision aligned Stonehenge (above), to midsummer sunset and midwinter moonset.

From stone to paper
The first writing was carved on stone or etched in wet clay. By 3500 B.C. the Egyptians invented papyrus, a writing material made by soaking shredded papyrus reeds and pressing them into a thick 'paper.' For long documents, sheets were sewn into a roll. Papyrus rolls were the main writing material for some 4,000 years. In c.200 B.C., parchment made from animal skins appeared, but did not become common until c.300 years later. About then, people began to sew sheets into book form instead of using unwieldy scrolls. A true paper, made of pulped rags, was invented c.2,000 years ago in China.

The 'White Death'
Scientists have shown that tuberculosis – nicknamed 'the White Death' last century – is caused by a microbe older than the human race. The earliest evidence of human victims comes from c.5000 B.C., when Egyptian carvings portray figures with tubercular spinal deformities. From the same period, the skeleton of a young male, found in Germany, reveals a rare bone form of the disease.

Ancient virus
The oldest known case of poliomyelitis was revealed by the deformed bones of an Egyptian mummy of c.3700 B.C. Later, polio was known to the Romans as a childhood ailment causing atrophy of the legs – 'the pestilence that is called lameness.' It was rarely fatal: polio did not become a major killer until last century, when modern hygiene prevented infants from developing immunity.

Miners' shrine ▼
In the Stone Age flint mines of Grimes Graves (below), eastern England, miners dug shafts into the chalk up to 39ft (12m) deep. An unproductive shaft became a shrine to the Mother Goddess. Its chalk carvings of the goddess and of a lifelike phallus were probably intended to encourage Mother Earth to bear the desired 'crop' of flints. The district preserves the tradition of flint knapping to this day: the nearby town of Brandon produces gun flints for export to U.S. flintlock buffs.

Lost lore of the Maya
The Maya of Central America wrote down their history and customs in books, with paper made from fig tree bark. In the 16th century, Spanish monks seeking to eradicate 'heathenism' destroyed these books so efficiently that today only three, plus one fragment, survive. Leader of the destruction, Brother Diego de Landa, wrote: 'As they contained nothing in which there were not to be seen superstition and lies of the devil, we burned them all, which they [the Mayan descendants] regretted to an amazing degree.'

SUPERFACTS

Biased burials
In Stone Age China, the Yang-shao culture had already developed a class-based society, with clear distinction between rich and poor. The wealthy lived in fine houses, and were given graves furnished with food, pottery, polished stone tools, and jade and shell jewelry. The poor buried their dead in simple pits. Women, whether rich or poor, had low status and were buried with little ceremony.

Practicing for war
Hunting skills were cultivated in ancient China as training for war.

The best hunting grounds were enclosed as game parks for the emperor's use. In c.1150 B.C. the Shang emperors established the 'Park of Intelligence,' near Peking. It covered c.15sq mi (40sq km) and was stocked with all manner of beasts and birds. The park was destroyed upon the fall of the last Shang emperor.

Military philosopher
The period of the Warring States (c.500-256 B.C.) in China produced the oldest known text on military philosophy, *The Art of War* by Sun Tzu Wu (active c.500 B.C.). It is studied by military personnel to this day. Chinese Communist leader Mao Tse-tung (1893-1976) took many of the guerrilla warfare directives in his 'Little Red Book' directly from Sun Tzu.

Recording myths
Greek myths were first set down in writing in c.500 B.C. by Hecataeus of Miletus.

The 'Great Traveler'
Han Dynasty China owed its new relations with the outside world to one man, the 'Great Traveler' Chang Chin. In 138 B.C. he made his first expedition, traveling north to the land of the Huns, where he was held captive for ten years. He escaped, with a Hunnish wife, and continued his journey, spending a year in Afghanistan and then another year as a Hunnish captive.

Root of all evil
Banking first appeared in Babylon c.1000 B.C., in the form of safekeeping, lending, and transfers. Coinage came later. The oldest known coins are electrum (gold and silver alloy) staters of Lydia, Turkey, dated to c.670 B.C., although the 'spade' money of the Chinese Chou dynasty may be earlier. The oldest surviving date-bearing coin comes from Sicily and is dated 'Year 1' (by our reckoning, 494 B.C.).

◄ Skull worship and headhunters
Many ancient cultures developed a cult of the human skull. The people of Jericho, Palestine, in c.7500 B.C., kept ancestors' skulls in their homes. They painted faces on the skulls and filled the eye sockets with shells. In Iron Age Europe, the Celts struck fear into their foes with their head cult. Enemies' heads were displayed outside homes and fortresses, as trophies of victory and to ward off evil. At the temple of Rocquepertuse, France (2nd century B.C.), skulls were mounted in niches in the stone doorposts (left). An honored foe might have his skull adorned with gold and used as a ceremonial drinking cup.

Greek scientists ▲ ►
Ancient Greek scholars laid the foundations of modern science. The mathematicians Pythagoras (right) (c.580-500 B.C.) and Euclid (c.330-275 B.C.) established many mathematical principles. Archimedes (c.287-212 B.C.) discovered specific gravity. Hipparchos (c.190-120 B.C.) cataloged the stars, calculated the equinoxes, and evolved a theory of the Sun's motion. Eratosthenes (c.276-194 B.C.) calculated the Earth's circumference with remarkable accuracy. Aristarchus of Samos (c.310-250 B.C.) first theorized that the Sun, not the Earth, is the center of our planetary system. Hippocrates (above) (c.460-377 B.C.), 'father of medicine', set a code of ethics for physicians which survives in the Hippocratic Oath taken by doctors today.

Perfect love
Greek philosophers such as Aristotle, boyhood tutor of Alexander the Great, taught that the highest form of love was 'perfect friendship' between two

males. This did not necessarily mean a sexual relationship: the 'Platonic ideal' of assexual devotion was held in greatest regard. However, many great men of the ancient world, including Alexander, appear to have been active bi-sexuals.

Washington, called from his plantation to command in the Revolutionary War, was named the 'American Cincinnatus,' and a group of his officers formed The Cincinnati, a society to help war widows and orphans. The city of Cincinnati, Ohio, founded as Losantiville, was renamed in their honor in 1790.

America's Roman hero
The favorite classical hero of the U.S.A.'s founding fathers was Lucius Quinctius Cincinnatus (c.519-438 B.C.). 'Called from the plow' to command a Roman army, he won a great victory; then refused political honors and returned to his farm. George

Long distance runner
The Marathon, the 26mi 385yd (42.2km) foot race of the modern Olympics, commemorates the feat of Pheidippides (Philippides), who in 490 B.C. ran 150mi (241km) in two days to ask Sparta to aid Athens at the battle of Marathon. (In another version of the legend, he ran some 26mi (42km) to bring news of victory to Athens, falling dead immediately afterwards.) The longest foot race at the ancient Olympics – where some were run in full armor – was probably of c.3mi (4.8km).

Galley slaves – and freemen ▲
In movies, Roman war galleys (above) are always manned by slaves chained to the oars. In fact, rather than fill warships with non-combatants, the fighting men took their turn at the oars, supplemented by a smaller number of condemned criminals – the true galley slaves. The galley also carried a square sail for wind power to supplement the oarsmen when necessary.

◀ Greek computer
The Antikythera Mechanism (left), a bronze gadget of the 1st century A.D., has been called 'an ancient Greek computer.' When it was found in 1959, in a wreck off the island of Antikythera, its complex workings – including geared wheels and a differential gear enabling two shafts to rotate at different speeds – baffled scholars. Recent studies suggest it was designed to calculate the past, present, and future motions of the Sun and Moon.

SUPERFACTS

Expensive army

The Mauryan Empire (c.320-185 B.C.) of India had a standing army said to have comprised 9,000 elephants, 30,000 cavalry, and 600,000 infantry. Its upkeep was a constant drain on the royal treasury and led to massive taxation.

Slave labor in publishing

Publishers in ancient Rome employed slaves to copy out manuscripts. One slave read out the book, while the others wrote it down. This method could lead to mistakes slipping in, but successful publishers like Titus Atticus (109-32 B.C.) built up a reputation for accuracy.

Ancestors of the brass band

Lurs, ritual wind instruments of Bronze Age Denmark, were the first 'brass' instruments. A few examples are so well preserved that they can still be played: huge curved horns, with a disk-shaped bell or mouth, and a range similar to that of a modern bugle. Their production shows superb craftsmanship, for they had to be cast without flaw in order to achieve correct pitch.

Underground shelters

Iron Age *fogous* in Cornwall, England, are large trenches, lined and roofed with stone and covered with earth to form underground refuges much like modern tunnel air-raid shelters. The small entrances would have been easily defended; at Halligye Fogou, where the 54ft (16.5m) main passage joins a secondary tunnel, there is a large, concealed rock projection to trip intruders.

Celtic 'women's lib' ▷

Celtic society had a degree of sexual equality unique among civilizations of the time. Women had full legal rights, not affected by marriage. They followed their men to battle and even joined in combat – classical writers said that Celtic women were even more to be feared than their husbands! The Romans in Britain were astounded to find women – like Cartimandua of the Brigantes, and Boudica (Boadicea) of the Iceni – recognized as tribal chiefs and military commanders. The cult of the Mother Goddess (above) remained central, and tribal deities, too, were as likely to be goddesses as gods.

Monster war machine

The most ambitious ancient war machine was the *Helepolis* ('City Taker') of the Macedonian leader Demetrius Poliocertes ('the Besieger') (d.283 B.C.). It was an armored, eight-storied, siege tower, c.140ft (43m) high, with catapults mounted at every level. Some 200 men manned a capstan-and-belt mechanism that enabled it to crawl forward on eight huge wheels (with the aid of c.3,000 more soldiers pushing). It was used in Demetrius's unsuccessful siege of Rhodes in 305 B.C.

First garden gnome

Wealthy Romans spent almost as much care and money on their gardens as on their villas. Marble sculptures and garden furniture, waterways and fountains, were displayed among symmetrical flowerbeds. One Pompeii garden contains a bronze fisherman dangling his rod into a fountain – ancestor of the modern garden gnome. In the later 1st century B.C. the fashion was for elaborate topiary, with trees clipped into the shape of animals, ships, or the letters of the owner's name.

Beaker burials ▽

The Beaker Folk, a mysterious people who appeared in Europe in c.2500 B.C., take their name from the bell-shaped beakers (below) buried with their dead (even including specially made miniature beakers for babies). The obvious importance of these drinking cups in their culture has produced the theory that they may have been the first European users of alcohol.

not wish their glory lessened by comparison with great predecessors.

◄ The Portland Vase

The Romans learned glass-working skills from the Syrians and Egyptians and went on to become masters of the craft. A supreme example is the Portland Vase (left), of the 1st century A.D. It is made of dark blue glass encased in opaque white glass: a design showing the story of the sea-goddess Thetis was cut from the outer layer so that the figures appear in blue. The Vase was on exhibition in London's British Museum when, in 1845, a lunatic smashed it into 200 pieces. It was carefully reassembled from a Wedgwood copy.

Empire for sale

Roman Emperor Commodus (ruled A.D. 180-193) was an insane tyrant who declared himself a god. The Praetorian Guard, a military elite, arranged his murder – and then auctioned off the throne. Highest bidder was Publius Helvius Pertinax, who lasted only three months before he too fell to a Praetorian hit man. Thereafter, several emperors (sometimes two or more at the same time) were 'elected' by the legions, having bought their allegiance with gold.

Child sacrifices ►

The Carthaginians sacrificed an average of 100 children per year to their gods Baal (right) and Tanit. In troubled years, as many as 500 infants were burned alive to pacify the gods, and the cremated ashes buried in the temple precincts. (Wealthy families may have offered up their younger children in the hope of avoiding later squabbles over inheritances.)

Caesar's calendar

Among Julius Caesar's social reforms was the introduction of the 'Julian Calendar,' the solar reckoning providing the basis of our modern system. The months were given their present number of days, and 'leap years' instituted. The month *Quinctilis* was renamed July in Caesar's honor (*Sextilis* would be renamed August after his successor). Pope Gregory XIII's 'Gregorian Calendar' of 1582 corrected errors in Caesar's system, but the Julian Calendar persisted in Britain until 1752; in Russia until 1918.

The fall of Maiden Castle

Europe's strongest Iron Age fort was Maiden Castle (Dorset, England). In c.350 B.C., Celtic tribesmen converted an abandoned Stone Age enclosure into a small stronghold. Some 300 years later it was refortified on a grand scale, with four lines of massive ramparts across which Celtic slingers hurled stones up to 100yd (90m). An ammunition dump of more than 20,000 stones was found behind the ramparts. The fortress fell to the Romans, probably c.45 A.D. A hastily dug mass grave near the eastern gates houses Celtic dead: a Roman iron dart is embedded in the spine of one skeleton.

Poison pen

Much of our knowledge of the personalities of earlier Roman emperors comes from the *Twelve Caesars* of Gaius Suetonius (c.A.D. 69-140). He says, for example, that Julius Caesar was a promiscuous bi-sexual; Tiberius, 'mud and blood,' a sadistic pervert; Claudius a driveling idiot, and so on. Like many early historians, he should be taken with a cellarful of salt. Most wrote to please patrons – in Suetonius's case, Emperor Hadrian – who did

INDEX

Page numbers in **bold** indicate major references including accompanying photographs. Page numbers in *italics* indicate captions to illustrations. Other entries are in normal type.

As penance for killing his family, Heracles performed 12 superhuman tasks (his 'Twelve Labors') – including fetching the three-headed hound Cerberus from Hell.

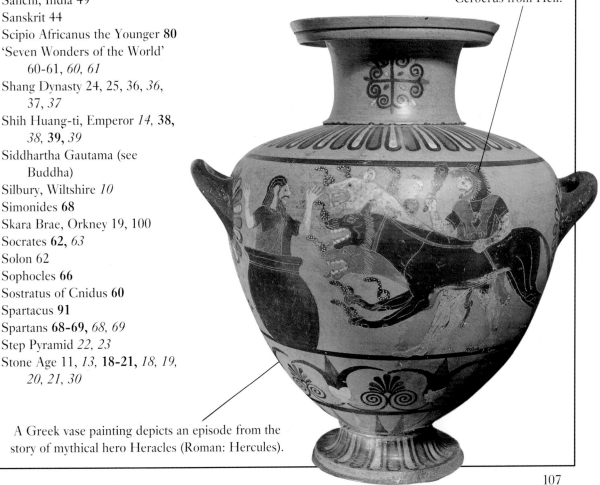

A Greek vase painting depicts an episode from the story of mythical hero Heracles (Roman: Hercules).

PICTURE CREDITS

The publishers wish to thank the following agencies who have supplied
photographs for this book. The photographs have been credited by page
number and, where necessary, by position on the page: B(Bottom),
T(Top), L(Left), BR(Bottom Right), etc.

Ancient Art & Architecture Collection: 6, 15,
19(BL), 19 (BR), 23(BR), 29(B), 38, 41(L),
44, 44-5, 54(B), 56-7, 60-1, 61, 63(BL),
67(B), 69(T), 71, 73(BL), 73(BR), 74, 74-5,
75, 80, 81, 82, 82-3(B), 83, 85(L), 85(C), 86,
86-7, 87(T), 92-3(T), 95(L), 95(R), 96-7(T),
9-97(B), 98, 98-9(T), 98-9(B), 101, 102, 103,
104(B), 105

Anthro-Photo File: 16, 16-17(T), 16-17(B),
31(R), 33(TR)

Art Resource: 5, 10(T), 11(L), 11(R), 12-13,
13, 18, 18-19, 23(T), 23(BL), 24(T), 24(B),
24-5, 25, 26(T), 26(B), 27(TL), 26-7(T),
26-7(B), 27(TR), 30(L), 30(R), 33(TL), 34,

36-7, 37(L), 41(R), 41(C), 42(B), 42(TL),
42(TR), 43(TL), 43(TL), 45(T), 45(B),
47(L), 48, 52, 52-3(T), 53(L), 53(R), 54(T),
54-5, 57(T), 57(C), (57(B), 58(T), 58(B),
59(TL), 60, 62, 63(T), 63(BR), 64(L), 64(R),
65(L), 65(R), 66-67, 67(T), 68, 68-9, 69(B),
70(T), 70(B), 70-1, 72, 76(T), 77(TL),
77(TR), 77(B), 78, 78-9, 79(L), 79(R),
82-3(T), 84, 84-5, 85(R), 87(B), 89(T), 89(B),
90, 91(B), 91(R), 94(T), 96, 97, 99, 100(T),
100(B), 104(T), 107

The Bettmann Archive: 28, 37(R), 66, 88(B)

Envision: 10(B), 40, 92, 94(B), 94-5

Lee Boltin: 32

North Wind Picture Archives: 28-9, 29(T)

Photo Researchers, Inc.: 2-3, 6-7, 12(B), 14,
17, 19(T), 20-1, 22-3, 30-1, 31(L), 33(B),
34-5, 35, 39, 42-3, 46-7, 51(R), 53(R), 55,
59(BL), 59(R), 62-3, 76(B), 77(TC), 88(T),
90-1, 92-3(B), 100-101

Woodfin Camp & Associates, Inc.: 8, 14-15,
20, 21, 36, 38-9, 40-1, 46, 47(R), 48-9, 49,
50, 50-1, 51(L), 72-3, 73(T)

Map artwork on pages 37, 49, 51, 54, 71, 77,
81, and 93 by Peter Bull.

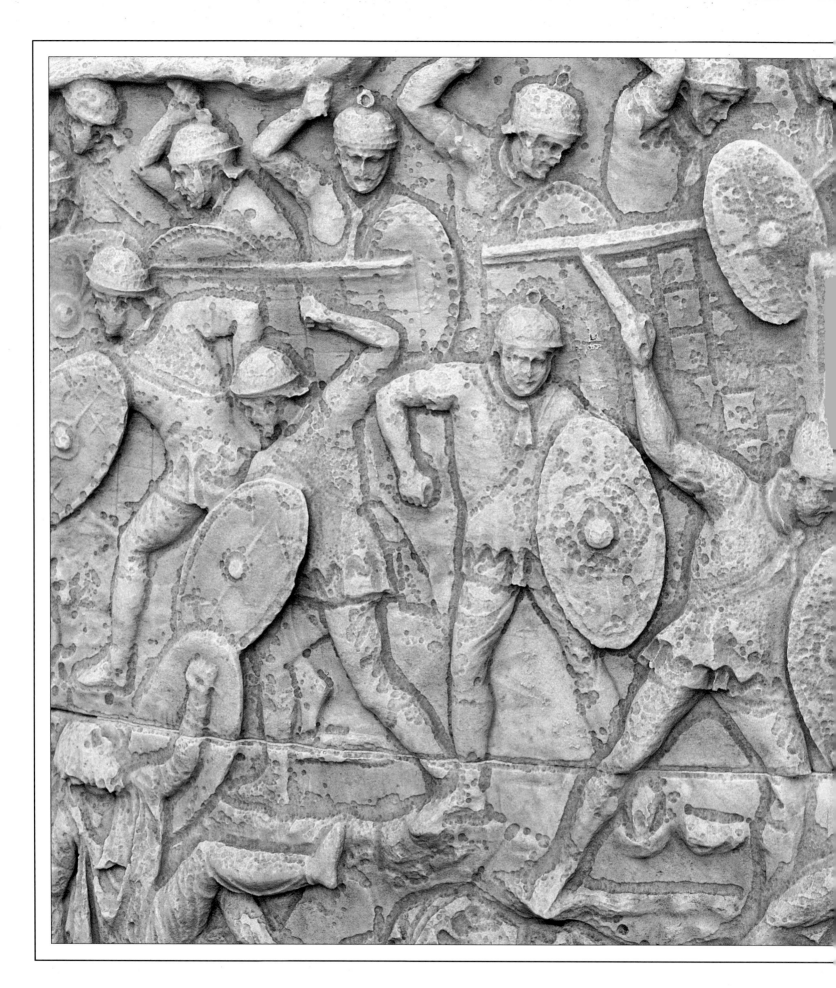